GOD SPEAKS

The Guidance of the Holy Spirit
in the
Book of Acts and Today

Personal Bible Study

JANET DECASTER PERRIN

GOD SPEAKS
The Guidance of the Holy Spirit in the Book of Acts and Today

Copyright © 2014, Janet DeCaster Perrin

Bibliography

Scripture marked NKJV is taken from the *New King James Version*. Copyright © 1982 by Thomas Nelson, Inc. Used by permission.

New Spirit-Filled Life Bible. Copyright © 2002 by Thomas Nelson, Inc.

The Harper Collins Bible Dictionary. Copyright © 1985, 1996 by The Society of Biblical Literature. All rights reserved.

Life Application Bible. Copyright © 1988 by Tyndale House Publishers, Inc. All rights reserved.

Text is from *The Living Bible* Copyright © 1971 owned by assignment by KNT Charitable Trust. All rights reserved.

Acts of the Holy Spirit: A Modern Commentary on the Book of Acts. Copyright © 1994, 1995, 2000 by C. Peter Wagner. All rights reserved.

Who's Afraid Of The Holy Ghost? Copyright © 1994 by Stevan F. Williamson. Reprinted by permission.

The Hayford Bible Handbook, Jack Hayford, Executive Editor. Copyright © 1995 by Thomas Nelson, Inc. Nashville, TN. All rights reserved.

Additional reference materials from various Bible teachers and mentors, including:

Dr. Alan and Rev. Dorothy Langstaff of Kairos Ministries (www.kairosmin.org).

Rev. Jim and Rev. Ramona Rickard of Resurrection Apostolic International Network (www.rainministries.org).

Rev. Jac and Bonnie Perrin, Senior Pastors of Eden Prairie Assembly of God (www.epassembly.org).

ISBN 10: 1-5059-1221-0
ISBN 13: 978-1-5059-1221-0

Additional Books

This book is also available as a TEACHER MANUAL, a ready-made guide that enables anyone to train and disciple others in the truth of Holy Spirit-empowered living. When paired with the companion STUDENT MANUAL, it provides all the tools needed to present this study in a small group, church Bible study, or Bible college classroom.

For additional copies of this or other books by Janet DeCaster Perrin, contact the author at **asamaritanwomanspeaks@gmail.com**, or go to **www.amazon.com/author/janetdperrin.**
Blog: **www.asamaritanwomanspeaks.com**   Twitter: **@janetDCperrin**

Book Editing/Design
Editing, cover design, and book design services were provided by Ronald Olson. He can be reached at ron@ronaldolson.com.

Table of Contents

Introduction

A question often asked in the Church today is this: "How does God communicate with people?" Perhaps you've asked that question yourself.

And why is it that some believers seem to have a stronger sense of what God is leading them to do? Do they have a heavenly telephone line on which God calls them? Do they hear a voice? Just how does God speak to us?

There is a plethora of non-Christian theologies out there today. In fact, many people claim to have had encounters with God or with the angelic realm. Some of these are real, but some are counterfeit. We must always use Holy Scripture as the ruler against which we measure such experiences. The Word of God is the starting place for any Christian who desires to pursue a deeper experience with God.

This study is a discipleship tool for Christians to grow into Holy Spirit-empowered witnesses, and our focus is to train Bible-believing Christians how to discern the leading of the Holy Spirit in their lives.

The Godhead (also referred to as the Holy Trinity) exists in three persons or unique personalities: God the Father, God the Son (Jesus Christ), and God the Holy Spirit. (See Luke 3:21-22.) Since the outpouring of the Holy Spirit's power on the Day of Pentecost, the third-person of the Trinity has been and remains the active agent of the Godhead in the earth. Jesus Christ, the Son of God, is seated at the right hand of the Father (Acts 1:1-10), and He sent the Holy Spirit upon believers on the Day of Pentecost (Acts 2:2-4). He continues to be the Baptizer in the Holy Spirit today.

When any individual comes to believe on the name of the Lord Jesus Christ according to Scripture, he is then saved (Romans 10:9) and indwelt with the Holy Spirit and is born again through faith, by God's grace. The believer is then qualified to receive the empowering baptism of the Holy Spirit to be a witness for Jesus in the earth (Acts 1:8).

The foundations and proof for this Pentecostal/Charismatic theology will be laid in the early chapters of this Bible study. Building upon that foundation, we will see how the Spirit-empowered believers in the early Church learned to discern and understand the ways in which God was communicating with them. In other words, He told them what to do, they did it, and their ministries bore much spiritual fruit.

The Book of Acts in the New Testament of the Holy Bible gives us many examples of how the Holy Spirit led the first Christians. It will be used as a type of training manual for the modern Christian who desires to receive the power to be a witness for Jesus Christ. As we study the experiences of the first Christians, we will use their model as a way to measure our experiences. God led them on missionary journeys and in their everyday lives. He continues to lead believers in the same ways today.

According to the Gospel of John, the Good Shepherd (Jesus) has a voice and He speaks to the hearts of his sheep (believers). (See John 10.) What John wrote about, the first Christians experienced. In addition to the guidance of His voice, the early Church was guided through dreams, visions, prophecy and circumstantially. They prayed in unity, were graced with the gifts of the Spirit, and the Holy Spirit led them in accordance with God's will. Today, many believers in the growing Pentecostal and Charismatic movements, across denominational lines, are experiencing that same guidance from the Holy Spirit.

GOD SPEAKS: The Guidance of the Holy Spirit in the Book of Acts and Today, was birthed out of the author's own journey to learn to discern and distinguish the Lord's guidance from that of the flesh or the devil. (The Bible is clear that believers must "test the spirits" as it tells us in 1 John 4:1-4.) As the Women's Pastor in her church, she was able to share what she learned with the women, and has taught the study as an adjunct faculty member to Bible college students.

If you choose to go through this Bible study with a partner, it is interactive and enables you to share and pray through the material together, and to practice what you are learning. This study is also available as a Teacher's Manual and a Student Manual, should you wish to share it in a group setting.

May God bless and guide you as you read and study His Word. May you come into a deeper revelation of His plan and purposes for your life. May His kingdom come and His will be done in your life!

Definitions: Gifts of the Spirit

Throughout this study we will be discussing the Gifts of the Spirit (as found in 1 Corinthians 12:4-11) and how they were displayed in the Book of Acts and how they are present in the lives of believers today. For clarification, here are the basic descriptions of each of the nine gifts.

Word of Wisdom

This gift is the ability to know the right steps to take in order to accomplish the will of God. It is receiving God's divine direction for what to do and what to say in any situation or to solve any problem. It often functions in conjunction with the Word of Knowledge. The difference is, the Word of Knowledge is informational, whereas the Word of Wisdom is instructional.

Word of Knowledge

This gift is manifested when the Holy Spirit reveals to an individual some information or truth about a person, a place, an event or situation. It can be facts about the past or present, and goes beyond anything the individual may already know.

Gift of Faith

This is the supernatural ability to believe and trust God completely, without doubt in His words and His faithfulness, no matter what kind of circumstances a person is facing. The Gift of Faith is a grace of the Holy Spirit that is beyond the faith that brings salvation.

Gifts of Healings

Referring primarily to physical sickness and disease, this is a miraculous healing that is beyond human ability or skill. Notice it refers to gifts in the plural. This Holy Spirit empowered gift can manifest in many different ways, such as through prayer or the laying on of hands and anointing with oil. The supernatural healing that occurs can be instantaneous or progressive.

Working of Miracles

This is the divine ability given to an individual in order to demonstrate the supernatural power of God over the ordinary course and laws of nature. When Jesus calmed the storms or turned water to wine, He was demonstrating this gift of the Holy Spirit.

Gift of Prophecy

Characteristics of New Testament prophecy are best described in 1 Corinthians 14:3, *"But he who prophesies speaks edification and exhortation and comfort to men."* This is a God-given word for a person that is meant to "build up" (edify), "stir up" (exhort), and "cheer up" (comfort).

Discerning of Spirits

This gift is the miraculous power to recognize activity in the spirit realm. It is the ability to discern between the demonic and angelic forces at work in a given situation. At times it is accompanied with a "spiritual insight" into the enemy's plans and purposes.

Different Kinds of Tongues

Speaking in tongues occurs under the inspiration of the Holy Spirit and the language and meaning is usually unknown by the person speaking. It could be a foreign language, a language that is no longer used in the world, or a supernatural spiritual language. It can be used privately in a person's prayer life, or used in a corporate setting if there is someone present who has the gift of Interpretation of Tongues.

Interpretation of Tongues

Interpreting tongues occurs when the Holy Spirit reveals to someone the meaning of a message given in tongues. This does not originate in the mind of man, but is of supernatural origin just like the Gift of Tongues or Gift of Prophecy. It is not necessarily a word-for-word translation, but a revelation of the meaning of the message.

Preface: One Way to Salvation

Before starting GOD SPEAKS: The Guidance of the Holy Spirit in the Book of Acts and Today, please read this important note from the author.

The First Step is Salvation

A common misconception in our society is the belief that good people who do good things will go to heaven when they die. The people who believe this are those who follow non-Christian religions, as well as some who occasionally or regularly attend churches, participate in religious activities, donate money to charitable or religious causes, or do other good works. They mistakenly assume that these activities will bring them to heaven.

That misunderstanding is a very serious one. In fact, it is the gravest mistake any person can make. The Bible is very clear that a person's works or good deeds can't earn them a trip to heaven. There is only one way to heaven and that is by faith in God through the Lord Jesus Christ. Here is a short teaching on this vital topic.

1. Sin Separates All People From God

Since the first man and woman made the choice to sin, all other people have had the same problem. We do things that are contrary to God's will, which is described in the Bible, and these sinful choices and actions separate us from a holy God.

> *Romans 3:23*
> *For all have sinned and fall short of the glory of God.*

> *Romans 6:23*
> *For the wages of sin is death, but the gift of God is eternal life in Christ Jesus our Lord.*

2. Turn Away From Sin and Toward Jesus

Since God understands that sin is a common problem for all of us, He has given us a way to receive His forgiveness and help. We are to confess our sins to God (admit that we have sinned) and repent (reject and turn away from our sins). But choosing to do that is left up to us. God does not force any individual into a relationship with Him. He invites us into a relationship with Him as a result of the sacrifice of His Son, Jesus Christ, and what He accomplished on the cross. He sent Jesus Christ to live on the earth and die on the cross as payment for the penalty of our sins. His free gift of forgiveness is available to every person.

> *1 John 1:9*
> *If we confess our sins, He is faithful and just to forgive us our sins and to cleanse us from all un-righteousness.*

3. One Way to Heaven

Jesus Christ said, "*I am the way and the truth and the life and no one comes to the Father except through Me*" *(John 14:6)*. Although popular culture tries to perpetuate the myth that there are many ways to heaven, and that all religions are equal, the Bible clearly states that there is only one way to heaven, and that is by faith in the Lord Jesus Christ. The offer of salvation is open to all, but Jesus is the only way.

> ### Acts 4:12
> *Nor is there salvation in any other, for there is no other name under Heaven given among men by which we must be saved.*"

4. Believe in Your Heart

Each person has to make a personal choice to confess their own sin, ask God for forgiveness, and put their faith and trust in the Lord Jesus Christ. It is a decision of the heart.

> ### Romans 10:9
> *If you confess with your mouth the Lord Jesus and believe in your heart that God has raised Him from the dead, you will be saved.*

5. Saved By Faith, Not Works

Good deeds, charitable giving, church attendance or good works of any kind cannot save any man or woman for eternity. If you've hoped that your good deeds will get you to heaven, you are hoping in vain. If you're trusting in your religious works to bring you salvation, you are trusting in vain. Placing your faith in Jesus Christ (a personal faith that comes from your heart) is the only thing that will get you to heaven. This gift of salvation is freely offered by God to everyone, and is available for you to-day.

> ### Galatians 2:16
> *Knowing that a man is not justified by the works of the law but by faith in Jesus Christ, even we have believed in Christ Jesus, that we might be justified by faith in Christ and not by the works of the law; for by the works of the law no flesh shall be justified.*

You don't need to have any question about whether your eternal destiny is heaven. You can be absolutely certain that heaven will be your home when your life on this earth ceases. Heaven is as close as a heartfelt prayer. If you have decided to follow Jesus, and you mean it with your whole heart, you can confirm your faith through this simple prayer.

Salvation Prayer

You can use your own words or pray a prayer like this in order to confirm your salvation.

> *"Father God, I admit that I have sinned against You in thought, word, and deed, both by things I have done and things that I have left undone. I ask You to forgive me and help me to change my sinful habit patterns. I believe that Jesus Christ is Your Son and that You sent Him as a sacrifice to pay the penalty for my sins. I now choose to accept the free gift of forgiveness and salvation that You have offered to me through Jesus Christ. Thank You for saving me."*

If you have put your faith and trust in the Lord Jesus Christ for the first time, I hope this book will be a helpful tool for you. May it help you grow strong in the Lord and in the power of His might!

Janet DeCaster Perrin

Like newborn babies, you must crave pure spiritual milk

so that you will grow into a full experience of salvation.

Cry out for this nourishment,

now that you have had a taste of the Lord's kindness.

1 Peter 2:2-3 (NLT)

Background of the Book of Acts
JESUS RECEIVES POWER

About This Study
- We will use the Book of Acts as a training manual for Christians.
- This study was birthed out of a directive the author received from the Lord to "teach them to hear My voice." The Holy Spirit stirred her heart to train Christians to look into Scripture to see how the Lord communicates with believers and brings revelation and impartation to the Church today.
- The Book of Acts is an example of how the disciples of Christ received His Holy Spirit and learned to pray and follow His guidance. That guidance came through His voice, through visions, dreams, circumstantial guidance, and in other ways. This is a study on how the first believers learned to discern the Holy Spirit's guidance, and how you can do it, too.
- This study is written from a Full-Gospel/Charismatic or Pentecostal perspective. (These are different names for similar movements within the Church.) It is not "that was then and this is now" theology, but rather our perspective is one of "that was then, and it is now, too!" Born-again believers can be baptized with the empowering Holy Spirit in the same way that the early believers were filled and can do the same works that they did, by the same Spirit.

Overall Study Theme
Jesus received the Holy Spirit's power to do His ministry. He then promised His disciples that power, they received it and did the same works that He did!

According to the *New Spirit Filled Life Bible* (NKJV), page 1489, "The Book of Acts is the story of the disciples receiving what Jesus received in order to do what Jesus did." It is a sequel to the Book of Luke by the same author who, according to Church tradition, was Luke, a Gentile physician.

In his commentary, *Acts of the Holy Spirit: A Modern Commentary on the Book of Acts*, page 17, C. Peter Wagner puts it this way: "The Gospel of Luke tells what Jesus did, and Acts tells what He expected His followers to do, both then and now. "

How did Jesus do His Father's works? How did the first disciples do it and how can you do it?

FOCUS POINT
Jesus received power from the Holy Spirit before beginning His earthly ministry.

Read Luke 3, 4; Matthew 4

KEY POINTS
1. Luke 3:16
   John the Baptist prophesies about the one to come who would baptize with fire and the Holy Spirit.
2. Luke 3:21-22
   The Holy Spirit comes upon Jesus at His baptism.

3. Luke 4:1
   Jesus being filled with the Holy Spirit.
4. Luke 4:14-22
   After overcoming Satan's temptation in the wilderness, Jesus returns in the power of the Holy Spirit and begins His public ministry.
5. Luke 4:18-19
   Jesus declares that He is the fulfillment of Isaiah's Messianic prophecy and proclaims what will be done in his ministry. The anointing of the Holy Spirit empowered Jesus (and now all believers following Pentecost) to:
   - Preach the gospel
   - Heal the brokenhearted
   - Proclaim liberty to captives (deliverance from demonic bondage)
   - Heal the sick
   - Set at liberty those who are oppressed

Focus Questions

1. What is the source of Jesus' power in His public earthly ministry?

   _____

   _____

2. List the specific things found in Luke 4:18-19 that the anointing of the Holy Spirit would empower Jesus to do.

   _____

   _____

   _____

3. List the things Jesus did after receiving the power of the Holy Spirit.
   Luke 4:15 _____
   Luke 4:30 _____
   Luke 4:31-32 _____
   Luke 4:33-36 _____
   Luke 4:38-39 _____
   Luke 4:40-41 _____
   Matthew 4:23 _____
   Acts 10:38 _____

Prayer

Father, I pray in Jesus' name, that You would give me the spirit of wisdom and revelation in order to understand Your Word. Open my understanding to comprehend Your love for me and Your purpose for my life. Help me to hunger and thirst after righteousness that I might be filled. Amen.

Personal Thoughts/My Response to What I Learned

_____

_____

_____

_____

_____

_____

_____

_____

_____

_____

_____

_____

_____

_____

_____

_____

Acts 1
JESUS PROMISES POWER

Introduction

In our first session we saw Jesus receiving the power of the Holy Spirit at his water baptism, and the works that He did following that experience. He taught in the synagogue, declaring himself to be the one prophesied in Isaiah 61. He went out preaching, healing and casting demons out of people wherever He went. Following His crucifixion, resurrection from the dead, and prior to His ascension to heaven, He then promised that the same power He had received would be given to His disciples.

FOCUS POINT

Jesus promised His disciples that they would receive the power of the Holy Spirit.

Read Acts 1

> Focus verses:
> Acts 1:4-8 (The promise of power.)
> Acts 1:9-11 (The ascension of Christ.)
> Acts 1:12-14 (The upper room prayer meeting.)
> Acts 1:24 (The prayer of agreement.)

Read Luke 24:44-49 (The promise of the coming Holy Spirit prior to His ascension.)

Read Mark 16:14-20 (The Great Commission prior to His ascension.)

The *New Spirit Filled Life Bible* (NKJV), page 1436, tells us the following:

> Jesus' instructions to the disciples before His ascension were clear – wait in Jerusalem and expect power. There was no hint given about what would happen, but clearly the evidence shows that Jesus knew what would occur and would make it abundantly clear to them. "The Promise of My Father" and all they experienced at the coming of the Holy Spirit on Pentecost are one and the same. As the Baptizer with the Holy Spirit (Luke 3:16), Jesus' instruction to His followers in Luke 11:13 to "ask" for the Holy Spirit and to wait until they receive power is pertinent to all believers for all times. All who believe are to ask and expect God to fill them with His Spirit and be empowered for their mission to serve Him. It is this supernatural power that Jesus uses to fulfill His mission to the world through His church.

KEY POINTS

1. Acts 1:1-8

    Jesus makes a promise that His disciples would receive power prior to His Ascension.

2. Acts 1:9-11 (The ascension of Jesus.)

Remember that our doctrine must be sound. Here we see the ascension of Christ after His bodily resurrection. He had promised His disciples power, and now after the ascension, we see the angels promise the return of Christ. Jesus Christ rose from the dead and ascended to heaven in the presence of witnesses prior to the outpouring of the Holy Spirit. (It is important to emphasize our belief in the bodily resurrection and ascension in order to distinguish Christianity from non-Christian cults.)

3. Acts 1:12-14 (The Upper Room Prayer Meeting.)
    Those praying in the upper room were in agreement together. Unity and agreement were an important part of the upper room prayer meeting.

    Notice that both men and women were in the upper room prayer meeting. From the beginning, women have been an important part of church fellowship.

Focus Questions

1. What did Jesus say about God's timing on His future return?

    _____

    _____

    _____

2. Why is the power of the Holy Spirit given and how is it to be used?

    _____

    _____

    _____

    _____

3. After Jesus' ascension, what was the first way that God chose to speak to His disciples?

    _____

    _____

    _____

4. Who was at the Upper Room prayer meeting? (Hint: men only, women only or both?)

    _____

5. What is the phrase that describes the relational situation in the upper room prayer meeting?

    _____

    _____

    _____

6. What was the first thing the Apostles did before they chose a replacement for Judas?

    _____

    _____

Prayer

Thank you, Jesus, that you received the power of the Holy Spirit to do Your earthly ministry, and that You went forth in that power preaching, teaching, healing the sick and delivering people afflicted with evil spirits. Thank you that You promised that same power to Your first disciples and to me, because of their (and my) faith in You. I ask You for that same power of the Holy Spirit now so I can be an effective witness for You wherever You send me – near or far. I pray for the power of the Holy Spirit to work in my life to heal me and set me free so I can witness to others and share Your Good News with them. Amen.

Personal Thoughts/My Response to What I Learned

Acts 2
JESUS SENDS POWER
Topics: Tongues, Interpretation of Tongues

Introduction
In our last session we saw that prior to His ascension Jesus promised His disciples that they would be endued with power from on high, and they were to wait for the Father's promise. In obedience, after witnessing the ascension of Jesus to heaven, the disciples (both men and women) returned to Jerusalem and held a prayer meeting that went on for several days. Prior to that meeting, the first way God chose to speak to the disciples was through a visitation by two angels who spoke to them and reassured them of Christ's return. The prayer meeting that they then held is known as the Upper Room prayer meeting. There they prayed together in unity and waited on the Lord. They made the important decision to choose Mathias as an apostle to replace Judas who had betrayed Jesus.

FOCUS POINT
It was on the Day of Pentecost that the Holy Spirit fell on believers.

Read Acts 2

Background of Pentecost
According to *The Living Bible,* p. 1619, Pentecost was held 50 days after Passover. Pentecost was also called the Feast of Weeks and Feast of Harvests. It was one of three major feasts of the year for the Jews set out in Leviticus 23:16, and was a festival of thanksgiving for the harvested crops. Jesus was crucified at Passover, and he ascended 40 days later. The Holy Spirit came 50 days after the crucifixion, 10 days after the ascension. Jews of many nations gathered in Jerusalem for this festival. Thus, Peter's Pentecostal sermon was given to an international audience.

KEY POINTS
1. Acts 2:1

   The upper room prayer meeting had gone on for several days and they were still in agreement.
2. Acts 2:2-13

   As the believers met together that day, suddenly there was a sound of a mighty, rushing wind, giving evidence of the presence of the Holy Spirit.
3. Acts 2:4

   The Gift of Tongues (speaking in other languages not known to the speaker) was the evidence of the outpouring of the Holy Spirit. The crowd was able to understand what was spoken as they heard their own languages.
4. Acts 2:14-39 (Peter's Pentecostal Sermon)

   Peter, after receiving the outpouring of the Holy Spirit accompanied by the Gift of Tongues, immediately stood up and preached the Gospel with great effect, and the result was 3,000 souls added to the Church.

5. Peter had received exactly what was promised in Acts 1:8 after his earlier cowardice and denial of Christ. He was restored by Jesus, then filled with the Holy Spirit, and thus empowered to proclaim Christ. Recall that Jesus also taught after receiving the Holy Spirit at His own water baptism.

Definitions: Gifts of the Spirit

Different Kinds of Tongues
Speaking in tongues occurs under the inspiration of the Holy Spirit and the language and meaning is usually unknown by the person speaking. It could be a foreign language, a language that is no longer used in the world, or a supernatural spiritual language. It can be used privately in a person's prayer life, or used in a corporate setting if there is someone present who has the gift of Interpretation of Tongues.

Interpretation of Tongues
Interpreting tongues occurs when the Holy Spirit reveals to someone the meaning of a message given in tongues. This does not originate in the mind of man, but is of supernatural origin just like the Gift of Tongues or prophecy. It is not necessarily a word-for-word translation, but a revelation of the meaning of the message.

FOCUS POINT
When the Holy Spirit came, His presence affected people in a discernible way.

KEY POINTS
Here is a summary of evidence of the Holy Spirit's outpouring on Pentecost.
1. Auditory Evidence
   A sound was heard of a mighty, rushing wind.
   Believers spoke in other tongues.
2. Visual Evidence
   Tongues of fire appeared over the believer's heads.
3. Other Evidence
   There was a boldness to preach and teach (confirming the promise in Acts 1:8).

FOCUS POINT
The Holy Spirit is God's "Church Growth Strategy!"

KEY POINTS
1. Acts 2:40-47
   The power of the Holy Spirit is at work and many people are added to the church daily. Many WONDERS AND SIGNS were done by the apostles, *"and the Lord added to the church daily those who were being saved."*
2. Notice the unity and agreement in prayer.

Focus Questions

1. List the ways (visible, audible, motivational) that the Holy Spirit's presence was manifested on the Day of Pentecost.

_____

_____

_____

_____

_____

2. According to Peter's Pentecostal sermon (quoting Joel 2:28-32), on whom will the Spirit be poured out in these last days? What will happen when the Spirit is poured out?

_____

_____

3. What happened to Peter immediately BEFORE he preached his Pentecostal sermon?

_____

_____

_____

4. What was the effect of Peter's sermon on his audience?

_____

_____

_____

_____

5. In verse 43, what did the apostles do?

_____

_____

_____

_____

Prayer

Father, pour Your Holy Spirit out on me. Jesus needed the Holy Spirit, the first disciples needed Him, and I need Him, too. Take anything from me that is not from You. I lay my past at Your feet, with all my failures, sins and mistakes, and I ask You to forgive me, cleanse me and fill me afresh with your Holy Spirit. Create in me a clean heart that I might be a useful vessel for You in my world, wherever You send me. Amen.

Personal Thoughts/My Response to What I Learned

_____

_____

_____

_____

_____

_____

_____

_____

_____

_____

_____

_____

_____

_____

_____

_____

_____

Acts 3
SPIRIT-EMPOWERED CHRISTIANS IN ACTION
Topics: Word of Knowledge, Healing

Introduction
In the first three lessons we laid a foundation for understanding the entire Book of Acts and the history of the outpouring of the Holy Spirit upon the first believers. It can be summarized this way.

JESUS RECEIVED POWER
In the first lesson we saw Jesus receiving power from the Holy Spirit, the third person of the Godhead. It was in the power of the Holy Spirit that Jesus did his earthly, public ministry.

JESUS PROMISED POWER
Prior to His ascension, Jesus promised His disciples that He would send them power from on high. (Found at the end of Luke and at the beginning of Acts.)

JESUS SENT POWER
On the day of Pentecost, Jesus sent the promised power from on high. He told the disciples they would be endued with power from on high, and He fulfilled His promise with the outpouring of the Holy Spirit. As they were together *"with one accord"* (in agreement), the disciples saw and felt a sound like a mighty rushing wind, and they began to speak with other tongues as the Spirit gave them utterance. A crowd of many nationalities heard them declaring the wonders of God in their own language. Peter got up in the power of the Holy Spirit and preached the first Pentecostal sermon and 3,000 were added to the Church. The believers were in unity, fellowship and prayer, and many signs and wonders were done by them.

As in Jesus' earthly ministry, after they were empowered by the Holy Spirit's outpouring at Pentecost, the disciples preached and did signs and wonders, including healing. In other words, they did the same things Jesus did!

Theme For Remainder of Study: *"Greater works than these shall you do."*
Just as Jesus moved in the power of the Holy Spirit, so did the early Church. We can learn to discern the leading of the Holy Spirit and be filled with His power today.

Most assuredly, I say to you, he who believes in Me, the works that I do he will do also; and greater works than these he will do, because I go to My Father (John 14:12).

Now the believers begin to do what Jesus prophesied in John 14:12. In Acts 3 we see Spirit-powered Christians in action!

FOCUS POINT
The disciples went about doing the same things Jesus had done.

Read Acts 3:1-12

Definitions: Gifts of the Spirit

Word of Knowledge
This gift is manifested when the Holy Spirit reveals to an individual some information or truth about a person, a place, an event or situation. It can be facts about the past or present, and goes beyond anything the individual may already know.

Gifts of Healings
Referring primarily to physical sickness and disease, this is a miraculous healing that is beyond human ability or skill. Notice it refers to gifts in the plural. This Holy Spirit empowered gift can manifest in many different ways, such as through prayer or the laying on of hands and anointing with oil. The supernatural healing that occurs can be instantaneous or progressive.

KEY POINTS

1. Acts 3:1-3 (Taking God-given opportunities in the marketplace.)
   Peter and John were on their way to a prayer meeting at the local synagogue when they came upon a hurting man. The lame man had been brought to a public place, the Beautiful Gate/Solomon's Porch, on the exterior of the temple. He was not in the temple, nor was he a believer. It was at this moment, in a public place, that they had a choice to make. How would they respond? Remember, they had just been baptized with the Holy Spirit.

2. Acts 3:4
   Peter and John said *"look at us."* It appears that the Holy Spirit was quickening the understanding of Peter that this man would be healed. This could have happened through a Word of Knowledge or the Gift of Faith. Somehow Peter discerned something when he looked at the man and received revelation from the Holy Spirit to pray for this particular man, knowing he would be healed.

   Compare this to Paul's revelation in Acts 14:8-10:
   And in Lystra a certain man without strength in his feet was sitting, a cripple from his mother's womb, who had never walked. This man heard Paul speaking. Paul, observing him intently and seeing that he had faith to be healed, said with a loud voice, "Stand up straight on your feet!" And he leaped and walked.

   Compare to Luke 5:17, when Jesus knew that the Holy Spirit's healing power was available at a specific moment.

3. Read 1 Corinthians 12:7-9 (NKJV), about the gift of the Word of Knowledge and the Gift of Faith.

   But the manifestation of the Spirit is given to each one for the profit of all: for to one is given the word of wisdom through the Spirit, to another the word of knowledge through the same Spirit, to another faith by the same Spirit, to another gifts of healings by the same Spirit...

   For an example of Jesus using a Word of Knowledge (supernatural revelation of a current or past event), read John 1:47-49 (NKJV).

Jesus saw Nathaniel coming toward Him, and said of him, "Behold, an Israelite indeed, in whom is no deceit!" Nathaniel said to Him, "How do You know me?" Jesus answered and said to him, "Before Philip called you, when you were under the fig tree, I saw you." Nathaniel answered and said to Him, "Rabbi, You are the Son of God! You are the King of Israel!"

For Deeper Study
Sensitivity to the Holy Spirit's presence and the Word of Knowledge

Jesus was sensitive to the Holy Spirit's anointing and what He wanted to do.

> In Luke 5:17, Jesus recognized *"...the power of the LORD was present to heal."*
> In Luke 6:8, Jesus *"knew"* the thoughts of the Pharisees.
> In Luke 8:46, Jesus said *"I perceived power going out from me."*

Here are some examples of the Word of Knowledge.

> Prior to encountering him, Jesus *"saw"* Nathaniel under a fig tree (John 1:47-49).
> Jesus had knowledge of the sinful lifestyle of the woman at the well (John 4:16-18).
> Jesus *"perceived"* their thoughts (Luke 5:22).

Definition of perceived: *epiginosko* (Strong's #1921)
Gnosis is the noun, *knowledge,* and ginosko is the verb, *to know.* Epigonosko is to know fully; to know with a degree of thoroughness, and competence to be fully acquainted in a discerning or recognizing manner. (From the *New Spirit Filled Life Bible,* NKJV, page 1395).

"The gift of the Word of Knowledge is the supernatural revealing by God to an individual of certain facts relating to people, places, events and/or situations. This gift always relates to either the present or the past. The key to this spiritual gift is supernatural (not natural) knowledge" (Stevan Williamson, *Who's Afraid of the Holy Ghost?*).

---

4. Acts 3:6-8

    Peter acted upon his faith, he took the man's hand and lifted him up, based upon the Word of Knowledge he'd had and the Gift of Faith he received. The lame man was divinely healed and walked. What was the result? Those in the public place were filled with *"wonder and amazement."*

5. Acts 3:12

    Peter seized His God-given opportunity to speak to the people about Jesus.

Read Acts 3:13-19

KEY POINTS

1. Peter preached the Gospel with boldness and without fear of man. He even accused his audience of putting Christ to death.

    The fear of man brings a snare, but whoever trusts in the Lord shall be safe (Proverbs 29:25).

Where did Peter get his boldness and zeal? From the Holy Spirit. (Review Acts 1:8; 2:2.)

2. Acts 3:16

    Notice that Peter gave all credit and glory to God. He didn't take the credit for himself.

3. Acts 3:19

    Peter called everyone to repent and be converted as the miraculous healing gave him the opportunity to preach the Gospel.

Focus Questions

1. While on their way to church, the disciples were confronted with a sick man outside the temple in the public marketplace who was in need of healing. What did they do? (Compare to Jesus' story of the Good Samaritan in Luke 10:25-37.)

    _____

    _____

    _____

    _____

2. What did Peter say to the man who needed healing? (Compare to Paul's statement in Acts 14:8-10.)

    _____

    _____

    _____

3. What type of supernatural revelation do you think Peter had in order to know that he was to pray for this particular man?

    _____

    _____

4. What action did Peter take as a result of what the Holy Spirit helped him to perceive?

    _____

    _____

    _____

5. After the man was healed by the Holy Spirit's power flowing through Peter, what did Peter do?

    _____

    _____

Prayer

Lord, I want to be sensitive to your Holy Spirit's leading in the course of everyday life like Peter was. Help me to be bold to act upon revelation that You give me, so I can be an effective witness for You. Thank You, Lord. Amen.

Personal Thoughts/My Response to What I Learned

Acts 4
STRETCHING OUT YOUR HAND TO HEAL
Topic: Boldness to Preach

Introduction

In the last session, we began to see the effect of the Holy Spirit upon the believers who had gathered in the Upper Room. On the Day of Pentecost they had received the outpouring of the Holy Spirit, which was accompanied by the sound of a mighty rushing wind, the appearance of tongues of fire resting upon their heads, and then the ability to speak in other tongues. As a result, they became Holy Spirit-filled Christians in action, doing the very same things Jesus had done after He received the Holy Spirit's empowerment. Jesus immediately preached and taught, healed and delivered people from demons as we saw in Luke 4. Now, the disciples of Jesus were filled with the Holy Spirit, boldly preached, and healed the sick.

We also saw Peter and John take pity on a lame man they encountered on their way to the temple to pray. They healed him by the power of the Holy Spirit as they prayed in a public place. Peter was a man of action. He received a Word of Knowledge and the Gift of Faith and Working of Miracles in the moment. He acted upon it, pulled the man up, and the lame man was instantly healed through the empowerment of the Spirit. Peter then saw his opportunity to preach and he preached the Gospel of Jesus Christ with great effect. In this session, we continue the story with Peter and John preaching in the marketplace.

FOCUS POINT
The Holy Spirit gives believers boldness to preach and withstand persecution.

Read Acts 4:1-4

KEY POINTS
1. Peter and John were arrested for preaching and healing a lame man. Despite the persecution that followed their boldness, many were converted.
2. Acts 4:4
   "...many of those who heard the word believed; and the number of the men came to be about five thousand." Five thousand new believers were converted to Christ due to the miraculous healing and preaching.
3. This fulfilled Jesus' promise in Acts 1:8. *"You shall receive POWER when the Holy Spirit comes upon you to be a WITNESS TO ME...."* The miracle opened their audience's hearts to receive Christ.

FOCUS POINT
God will use ordinary people to do extraordinary miracles.

Read Acts 4:5-31

KEY POINTS
1. Acts 4:8 (Peter's empowerment.)
   Peter was filled with the Holy Spirit before he spoke.
2. Acts 4:10 (Peter's humility.)
   This is a model for us in healing prayer. Peter takes no credit for himself, but instead gives credit to Jesus. When you pray for the sick and Jesus heals them, give Him credit and give Him glory
3. Acts 4:13 (God uses the ordinary.)
   Are you uneducated and untrained? Great! Then you qualify to serve Jesus. You can have the same Holy Spirit power and boldness given to Peter and John so you can preach in the streets and public places, heal the sick and perform miracles. God uses the ordinary! That's good news.
4. Acts 4:14
   Healing is a sign to confirm the Gospel. The religious leaders arrested Peter and John, but the healed man standing by them proved their point – Jesus is the Christ of God, and mighty miracles of compassion occur in His name.
5. Acts 4:22
   The healed man was over 40. Young or old, it's never too late to accept God's grace and mercy.
6. Acts 4:29-31
   The disciples were filled <u>again</u> with the Holy Spirit subsequent to being baptized with the Holy Spirit on the Day of Pentecost.

Personal Application
Ponder and meditate on Acts 4:13.
Who does God choose to use? What does that mean for your life?

For Deeper Study
Acts 4:19-20
Read Peter and John's words and compare to these verses:
     Proverbs 29:25 (The fear of man brings a snare.)
     Psalm 111:10 (The fear of the Lord is the beginning of wisdom.)
     Ask God to reveal to you any areas where you struggle with the fear of man.

"Now, Lord, look on their threats and grant to Your servants that with all boldness they may speak Your word, by stretching out Your hand to heal and that signs and wonders may be done through the name of Your holy Servant Jesus.' And when they had prayed, the place where they were assembled together was shaken; and they were all filled with the Holy Spirit, and they spoke the word of God with boldness" (Acts 4:29-31).

Notice that they were initially baptized in the Spirit on the Day of Pentecost and here they are filled again. An old Pentecostal saying is, "One baptism, many fillings."

Peter's Prayer for Boldness

After being released from custody, Peter and John don't shrink back and become slaves again to fear. Peter had done that previously when he denied Christ and he wasn't about to do it again. He had learned from his mistake; he knew who he was and Whose he was, so he cried out to God in prayer.

> *"Now, Lord, look on their threats and grant to Your servants that with all boldness they may speak Your word, by stretching out Your hand to heal and that signs and wonders may be done through the name of Your holy Servant Jesus.' And when they had prayed, the place where they were assembled together was shaken; and they were all filled with the Holy Spirit, and they spoke the word of God with boldness" (Acts 4:29-31).*

Focus Questions

1. Why were Peter and John arrested?

   _____

   _____

   _____

   _____

2. Who arrested Peter and John?

   _____

   _____

3. What was the result of their preaching?

   _____

   _____

   _____

4. What was Peter filled with before he preached?

   _____

   _____

   _____

5. To whom did Peter give credit for healing the lame man?

   _____

   _____

6. What hindered the religious leaders from locking up Peter and John and throwing away the key? (Hint: The healed man makes the point in verse 14 and the people make the point in verse 21.)

   _____

   _____

   _____

Prayer

Heavenly Father, forgive me for those times that I fear man, and don't speak for You when You are prompting me. Forgive me, cleanse me, and heal me. Thank You for Your grace and mercy, which I receive along with Your forgiveness now. Make me more sensitive to Your Holy Spirit so that I discern Your promptings and Your guidance. Lord, apart from You I can do nothing. Please give me boldness from Your Holy Spirit to love the lost and dying people in my world, and to share my faith in You in whatever way You prompt me to speak. Help me to see the crippled beggars that You put in my path on the way to church, be they hurting housewives, broken children, people who are sick, or war-weary Christians. Set me free from bondage to religion, so I can move according to Your compassion and in the power of the Holy Spirit. I surrender my mouth and lips to You, as well as my hands and feet, for you created them. Use me Lord, just as I am. Amen.

Personal Thoughts/My Response to What I Learned

Acts 5
BE SURE YOUR SIN WILL FIND YOU OUT
Topics: Prophecy, Word of Knowledge

Introduction

In the last chapter, we saw two disciples arrested, threatened, then set free after being taken into custody for healing a lame man. Instead of giving up in defeat, they prayed together in unity for more boldness from the Holy Spirit. In Acts 4:31, the place where they were praying together was shaken and they were all filled with the Holy Spirit and spoke the word of God with boldness. That leads us to Acts 5. It is a sobering chapter to read, but it should advise us all that we need to take our faith seriously, and have a healthy respect for God and for His Church. As it says in Proverbs, *"The fear of the Lord is the beginning of wisdom."*

FOCUS POINT

We reap what we sow. Right moral choices are an integral part of our faith.

Read Acts 5:1-11

C. Peter Wagner in his commentary, *The Acts of the Holy Spirit: A Modern Commentary on the Book of Acts* (pages 117-119), points out that "Ananias and Sapphira made a conscious decision to lie. They had a number of choices in the situation, and they made a deliberate choice to lie. We cannot use the excuse "the devil made me do it" as moral choices are ours to make. Despite direct assaults from the enemy, Job chose to do what was right and Ananias and Saphira could have done the same."

Personal Application

What does this tell you about the importance of honesty and forthrightness in the Body of Christ and in your own life?

FOCUS POINT

The Holy Spirit can use revelatory gifts to cleanse the Church.

KEY POINTS

1. Peter had revelation from the Holy Spirit of Ananias' and Sapphira's sin and God used it to cleanse the church. The Word of Knowledge revealed Ananias' secret sin of keeping back part of the proceeds of the sale of the land. His lying was exposed through revelation.

2. Acts 5:9

   After confirming that Sapphira had conspired in the lie, Peter then prophesied her death. Remember, Peter held an Ephesians 4:11 ministry office and this is not the normal usage of prophecy.

For Deeper Study

Read the following Scriptures regarding revelation gifts.

- 1 Corinthians 14:24-25 (The Gift of Prophecy reveals secrets of the heart.)
- 1 Corinthians 12:8-11 (The gifts of the Spirit include the revelation gifts: Word of Knowledge, Word of Wisdom and Gift of Prophecy.)

Definitions: Gifts of the Spirit

Word of Knowledge
This gift is manifested when the Holy Spirit reveals to an individual some information or truth about a person, a place, an event or situation. It can be facts about the past or present, and goes beyond anything the individual may already know.

Gift of Prophecy
Characteristics of New Testament prophecy are best described in 1 Corinthians 14:3, *"But he who prophesies speaks edification and exhortation and comfort to men."* This is a God-given word for a person that is meant to "build up" (edify), "stir up" (exhort), and "cheer up" (comfort).

FOCUS POINT
The Gospel is confirmed with signs and wonders.

Read Acts 5:12-16

KEY POINTS
1. Jesus had a ministry accompanied by signs and wonders – healings, miracles, deliverance, etc. He had promised His disciples power. They received that power on the Day of Pentecost (and were refilled with the Spirit's power again in prayer) and now they were doing the same things He had done.
2. Acts 5:15
   Peter's shadow healing people is an example of the anointing (the power and presence of the Holy Spirit) manifesting and moving in a crowd, even without the laying on of hands.
   Compare this to Luke 6:17-19 and Luke 8:46, when power went out from Jesus.

Where Was This In Jesus' Ministry?
Compare and notice that Acts 5:15 is similar to Luke 6:17-19 and Luke 8:46. The manifest power had gone out from Peter's shadow in the same way it had gone out from Jesus. The anointing was invisible, but tangible, and Jesus could sense when the anointing went out from Him.

FOCUS POINT
God uses angels to communicate with believers.

Read Acts 5:17-21

KEY POINTS
1. An angel appeared, spoke to them, and released them from jail.
2. It is worth noting the characteristics of this angelic encounter.

   The angel had the physical ability to open doors.

   The angel had a voice and he spoke and gave directions.

   The holy angels never accept man's worship. (This is a key distinction between a holy angel and a fallen angel, also known as a demonic spirit.)
3. According to the *New Spirit Filled Life Bible* (NKJV) page 1499 notes to Acts 5:19:

   There are more direct references to angels in the NT than in the OT. Jesus talked about angels (Matthew 26:53; Mark 13:32; Luke 20:34-36; John 1:51) and not only were angels in attendance at His birth, resurrection, and ascension, they were active amid the early church's life. In Acts, angelic activity:
   1. Freed apostles imprisoned for their faith – (12:6-7)
   2. Led Philip to an evangelistic opportunity – (8:26)
   3. Told Cornelius how to find Peter in order to hear the gospel – (10:3-5)
   4. Struck judgment on wicked Herod – (12:23)
   5. Encouraged Paul caught in a killer storm – (27:23)

   Throughout the New Testament, believers are given instruction on the presence, nature and function of angels, fallen and unfallen.

For Deeper Study

Read the following Scriptures to learn more about angels in the New Testament.

Matthew 26:53	Acts 10:3-5	Colossians 1:16
Mark 13:32	Acts 12:6-7	Hebrews 1:14
Luke 20:34-36	Acts 12:23	1 Peter 1:12; 3:22
John 1:51	Acts 27:23	2 Peter 2:4
Acts 8:26	Ephesians 6:12	Revelation 5:11-12

Recommended supplementary reading: *Angels* by Billy Graham.

Note: There is a great deal of non-Christian teaching on angels, so it is particularly important to study what the Bible says about angels.

FOCUS POINT
The Holy Spirit gives believers perseverance.

Read Acts 5:22-32

KEY POINTS
1. On trial again, the apostles continued to speak the word of God boldly and did not give up. It is a

lesson for us in perseverance.

2. Being baptized (and refilled) with the Holy Spirit imparts boldness to believers, an aspect of which is perseverance and persistence. These are key character traits for the maturing Christian to develop.

3. Compare this to the Parable of the Persistent Widow in Luke 18:1-8.

Personal Application

Compare this to Jesus' instructions on prayer found in Luke 18:1-8. According to that parable, should we quit when we don't see results of our prayers right away or continue to pray? How should this encourage your personal prayer life?

Focus Questions

1. How is the revelation of Ananias' and Sapphira's sin an example of Numbers 32:23?

2. Where did Ananias and Sapphira go wrong?

3. Could they say, "the devil made me do it," or did they choose to do the wrong thing?

4. How was the sin of Ananias and Sapphira discovered?

5. What gift did the Holy Spirit most likely use to communicate to Peter?

6. According to verse 14, what was the result of the signs and wonders?

7. How does the ministry described in Acts 5:12-16 partially fulfill what Jesus said in His last words in Acts 1:8?

_____

_____

_____

8. What did the angel do and say and what was the apostles' response?

_____

_____

_____

9. Does God use angels as an instrument of communication and deliverance for followers of Jesus Christ?

_____

_____

10. Do you think that being filled with the Holy Spirit gave the disciples persistence and perseverance? Why or why not?

_____

_____

_____

_____

_____

Prayer

Father, I pray in the name of Jesus that You would fill me with the Holy Spirit anew today. I pray that I would have the same boldness as the first disciples did, and that I would have persistence, tenacity and good moral character. Keep me from the evil of lying and other moral wrongdoing. May I be quickly convicted in my heart should I sin against You so that I will not fall into the trap of deception that Ananias and Sapphira did. Thank you Lord that when I repent, You forgive my sins and cast them as far as the east is from the west. Protect me from the traps of the evil one. I ask You to cover me in the blood of the Lord Jesus Christ and to surround me with Your hedge of protection. I pray that I would always pray and that I would never, never, never, never, never give up! Amen.

Personal Thoughts/My Response to What I Learned

_____

_____

_____

_____

_____

_____

Acts 6 & 7
MIRACLES MINISTRY SPREADS
Topics: Spiritual Leadership, Visions

Introduction

Through the story of Ananias and Sapphira in our last session, we saw the need for integrity and moral character in our walk of faith. We also saw an example of Jesus using Peter, through one of the revelatory gifts of the Holy Spirit, to perceive what was in the hearts of Ananias and Sapphira. God used that gift of revelation to protect and cleanse the church. We saw the disciples once again being filled with the Holy Spirit and going forth proclaiming the word of God with boldness. They persevered in their task despite being put on trial. Perseverance and tenacity were the result of what the disciples received from the Holy Spirit. They were empowered and they didn't give up in the face of adversity.

In this session, we will study two chapters, focusing on the results of being filled with the Holy Spirit. We will also look at how the Holy Spirit chose to communicate and continues to communicate with the believers. Remember that Hebrews 13:8 says, "*Jesus is the same yesterday, today and forever.*" Therefore, believers today can have the same boldness and tenacity, and do signs and wonders, after we are born-again and baptized with the Holy Spirit. We can develop an intimate relationship with God through prayer, reading the Bible and spending time listening to Him. Out of an intimate relationship with Jesus Christ and a heart of integrity will come the ability to perceive the Holy Spirit's guidance.

FOCUS POINT

Church leadership, including oversight of administrative tasks, should come from the morally upright who are full of faith and the Holy Spirit. Non-apostolic leaders, full of the Holy Spirit, can and should go out preaching. Signs and wonders will follow their ministry in the public marketplace.

Read Acts 6:1-15, Acts 7

Background

A conflict arose among a bi-cultural group of Hebrew (Judean) Jews, Galilean Jews and Greek-speaking (Hellenist) Jews. (The believers were all still Jews at this point, as the Gentile mission had not begun.) In short, there was a disagreement in the church. (They were not referred to as "Christians" until later, nor was there a "church" yet.) They were quarreling about how the benevolence ministry of food distribution to the widows should be handled, as the Hebrew widows and the Hellenist widows were not being treated the same.

KEY POINTS

1. Acts 6:2

    The apostles decided they must focus their time on ministry of the Word and prayer and they needed administrative help. They needed the individuals God chose, and in so doing, they needed to overcome their own prejudices (Hellenist v. Hebrew). God chooses spiritual leaders, while other leaders recognize and develop their potential.

2. Acts 6:3

    They chose people of 1) *good reputation*, 2) *full of the Holy Spirit and* 3) *wisdom*.
    C. Peter Wagner's commentary, *The Acts of the Holy Spirit, pp 150-151*, disagrees with these seven
    being the first "deacons," as many commentators suggest. These seven were chosen for this spe-
    cific administrative task of food distribution, but they were not "subordinates." They quickly be-
    came preachers and missionaries in their own right, in addition to handling the important task they
    were given of overseeing food distribution. The benevolence ministry was very important in the
    early church.

3. Acts 6:5

    Stephen was chosen because he was full of 1) *faith* (probably the spiritual Gift of Faith, beyond
    saving faith), and 2) *the Holy Spirit*.

4. Acts 6:6

    Hands were laid upon them to impart and activate gifts of leadership.

5. Acts 6:7

    As a result, the word of God spread and the disciples *multiplied*.

6. Stephen becomes the focus of the narrative.

    He is described as a man full of faith and power. He is not an apostle, but is recognized by the
    apostles for his faith, he is anointed for administrative tasks and leadership, and he also preaches
    with signs following.

7. Acts 6:10

    Stephen reasons with a group from a synagogue and even those who accuse Stephen of blasphemy
    are "*not able to resist the wisdom and the Spirit by which he spoke.*"

8. A continuation of a theme.

    The original pattern of Jesus receiving power from the Holy Spirit and preaching with signs and
    wonders following the Word, is continued here. The apostles received the same promised power
    from the Holy Spirit and preached with signs and wonders. Now as the believers are being multi-
    plied, others are recognized for their faith, and non-apostolic leaders are put over administrative
    tasks, such as mercy ministries. The impartation of an anointing for leadership came upon them as
    the apostles prayed for them.

9. Acts 7

    Stephen, the man full of faith and the Holy Spirit, steps out in boldness and preaches the Gospel.
    Using the word of God, his knowledge of the Scriptures and under the anointing of the Holy Spirit,
    he gives a recount of the history of Israel. He is a Jew, relating to his Jewish audience, and sharing
    Jesus Christ with Jews, calling them to faith in the Messiah. Stephen's sermon prior to his death is
    an excellent resource in summarizing the Old Testament history of Israel.

FOCUS POINT

The Holy Spirit sometimes communicates to believers visually and opens their eyes to "see" in the
realm of the Spirit.

Read Acts 6:15, Acts 7:55-56

Read in conjunction with Exodus 34:29-30; Acts 2:14-21; Joel 2:28-32.

KEY POINTS

1. Acts 6:15

   Visual communication is one of the ways the Holy Spirit guides us. Even the non-believers see Stephen's face as that of an angel.

2. Compare to Moses.

   In the Old Testament (Exodus 34:29-30), Moses had a "shining" face that others could see.

3. Acts 7:55

   Stephen said he could *"...see the heavens opened and the Son of Man standing at the right hand of God."*

Word Usage

According to the *New Spirit Filled Life Bible* (NKJV), page 1480, the Greek word for the English translation *see* is *theoreo,* which means "to behold, view attentively, perceive, look with a prolonged and continuous gaze. *Theoreo* conveys looking with a purpose, with interest, and with close scrutiny." Note that in John 20:14, *theoreo* is also used. In that passage it says, *"she turned around and saw Jesus standing there and Jesus said to her, 'Woman why are you weeping?'"*

In Acts, Stephen *saw* into heaven, as clearly as the woman *saw* Jesus standing there. This kind of insight comes from the Holy Spirit

Testimonies of "Seeing in the Spirit."

Rev. Ramona Rickard of RAIN Ministries teaches that part of the way the Holy Spirit uses her in a meeting, is to "see" what the Holy Spirit is doing. She will see a faint glow around someone's head (much like Stephen's shining face), then she'll know in her spirit to whom the Holy Spirit wants her to minister. I believe what she is seeing is the anointing – the manifest power and presence of the Holy Spirit.

Dr. James Maloney, a 21st century healing evangelist, sees what he calls the "dancing hand of God" upon people in meetings, and those are the ones whom he prays for and they receive miraculous creative miracles.

Testimony of the Author

Sometimes in prayer I will receive pictures or visions of situations or particular answers to my prayers, or prophetic revelation that come as pictures in my minds eye. On one Sunday in my home church, I was in the front row praying and worshipping prior to the altar ministry time, and the Lord gave me a quick vision of a certain woman who would come forward. The vision was a type of Word of Knowledge. I knew what the woman would look like and what kind of healing she needed. Since I am on the church's altar team, I felt I should pray at the altar that day.

The first lady who came had a different need and looked different than my vision. But on faith, I kept waiting for the lady in the vision and about five minutes later she came forward to receive ministry and was healed of some emotional issues. God is so good!!

One way He communicates to His people is through visual means as it says in Acts 2:14-21 (quoting Joel 2:28-32), *"I will pour out of My Spirit on all flesh: Your sons and your daughters shall prophesy. Your young men shall see visions, your old men shall dream dreams. And on my menservants and on my maidservants I will pour out My Spirit in those days and they shall prophesy."*

For Deeper Study
Seeing in the realm of the Spirit

Visual communication is one of the ways the Holy Spirit guides us. He can even open the eyes of non-believers in special circumstances. Read 2 Kings 6:8-23.

Pray for yourself like Elisha prayed in verses 16 and 17: *"Lord, open his eyes that he may see"* (NKJV).

Read and pray through the Apostle Paul's prayer in Ephesians 1:15-23. Write down any personal reflections on this prayer as you pray it daily. Share any personal testimonies of how God opens your spiritual eyes.

FOCUS POINT
Forgiveness is vital in the life of every believer.

Read Acts 7:59-60

KEY POINTS
1. Stephen is stoned to death for preaching Jesus as the Christ.
   While he is being stoned, he cries out, "*Lord, do not charge them with this sin.*" And then he dies. This is reminiscent of Christ's words at his Crucifixion in Luke 23:34.
2. The importance of forgiveness in our Christian walk cannot be overemphasized.
3. It was the religious people who put Jesus on the cross. The religious people stoned Stephen to death. Today we must be aware that people are being literally stoned by religious zealots in the Middle East. We can be figuratively stoned in our Western churches through bad behavior by others at church who do not accept the work of the Holy Spirit. We must be quick to forgive offenses.
4. We are commanded in the Lord's Prayer to forgive. (See Matthew 6:12-15.)

Focus Questions
1. In Acts 6:4, on what were the Apostolic leaders to focus their duties?

   _____

   _____

   _____

   _____

2. What were the qualifications given in Acts 6:3 for choosing leaders over the ministry of food distribution for the widows?

_____

_____

3. What were Stephen's qualifications for ministry as listed in Acts 6:5?

_____

_____

_____

4. What did Moses' face "look" like in Exodus 34:29-30?

_____

5. What was the appearance of Stephen's face like in Acts 6:15?

_____

6. What did Stephen see or perceive in Acts 7:55-56?

_____

_____

_____

7. How do Stephen's words compare to the words of Jesus in Luke 23:34?

_____

_____

_____

8. Compare these words to Jesus' instructions in the Lord's Prayer found in Matthew 6:12-15. What does this say to you about the importance of forgiveness?

_____

_____

_____

_____

Prayer

Father, I pray now in the name of Jesus and I ask you to bring to mind anyone that I need to forgive. Cleanse my heart and renew a right spirit within me. Let me be like your Son, by the power of the Holy Spirit, and say, "Father, forgive them, for they know not what they do." I choose now, by the Holy Spirit, to lay down any offenses that I have received from those who may have hurt me. I ask for your power to forgive and be healed in my emotions and set free in my spirit in the name of Jesus. Father, help me to bring these things up, out and onto the cross of Christ and leave them there. I pray now in Jesus' name that you would refill me with your Holy Spirit, and that you would open my spiritual eyes *to see in Jesus' name. Father, send a spirit of wisdom and revelation in the knowledge of You, that the eyes of my understanding would be enlightened. I pray that I might be a more effective witness for You in my home, in my church, in my community and in the marketplace. Amen!*

Personal Thoughts/My Response to What I Learned

_____

_____

_____

_____

_____

_____

_____

_____

_____

_____

_____

_____

_____

_____

_____

_____

_____

Acts 8
HELLO, THIS IS GOD
Topic: Discerning of Spirits

Introduction

Stephen's bold and zealous sermon in chapter 7 of Acts drew a bright line for his Jewish audience between the old order of Jewish temple worship and the new order of coming to God directly through the Messiah, the Lord Jesus Christ. Through the power of the Holy Spirit, Stephen boldly made his case for Christ, and fierce persecution came against him and became the order of the day for believers thereafter. Stephen's eyes were opened in the realm of the Spirit, he saw Jesus stand up at the right hand of God and he was brutally murdered for his faith. He became the first martyr of the Church and went to his death praying for forgiveness for his persecutors.

In chapter 8 we are introduced more fully to Saul of Tarsus, a Pharisee who is an enemy of the Church and has consented to Stephen's death. The persecution of the Church leads to a scattering of the disciples throughout the region. The apostles remain in Jerusalem, but the rest, who have been filled with the Holy Spirit, go out preaching.

FOCUS POINT
Spirit-filled believers preach the Word and signs, including healing and deliverance, follow.

Read Acts 8:4-8

KEY POINTS
1. Persecution scatters the disciples, they preach the Word and signs follow.
2. Introducing Philip the evangelist. This Philip, like Stephen, is not one of the apostles. The apostle Philip was a Hebrew Jew who remained at Jerusalem. Our Philip is the first specifically recognized evangelist. He was a Hellenist Jew, and as such, is the first cross-cultural minister as he goes to the mixed-race Samaritans. (See Acts 21: 8-9 where he is called *"Philip the evangelist who had four virgin daughters who prophesied."*) According to John 4:9 study notes in the *New Spirit Filled Life Bible,* the Samaritan race resulted from the Assyrians inter-marrying with Jews. Therefore, there was a historical enmity between Samaritans and Jews.
3. The Samaritan Mission begins.
   Jesus had laid the foundations for the Samaritan mission when he spoke to the woman at the well. (See John 4:35.) By doing so, he broke with tradition not only by reaching out to a sinful woman, but one from a historically hated people group.
4. People listened to the Gospel spoken by Philip and *"heeded"* his words when they saw *"miracles and many who were paralyzed and lame were healed and unclean spirits came out with shrieks."* Revival broke out in Samaria despite the historical prejudice. Philip preached Christ and God confirmed the Gospel with miracles.

FOCUS POINT
Spiritual warfare is real, and people (individuals and whole groups) can be bound and deceived by Satan through sorcery and witchcraft. The power of the Holy Spirit can set them free if they repent of their sin.

Read Acts 8:9-13

KEY POINTS
1. Here is a classic illustration of the difference between witchcraft or sorcery and Christianity. Simon the Sorcerer is a self-exalting controller who wields control over people's souls and minds through demonic powers. He claims greatness in himself, and is a very prideful, wicked man. Looking carefully at Acts 8:9-10, it seems from the text that a whole city was under the power of some occult force connected with this man, Simon.
2. Philip the evangelist then comes preaching Christ in the power of the Holy Spirit. Healings, miracles and deliverance happen. People, previously bound, are set free and accept Christ. They are converted and water baptized. Simon also is converted to Christ and is baptized in water.
3. Look again at Acts 8:8. It says there was *"great joy in that city"* as a result.

FOCUS POINT
God gives gifts of revelation to Holy Spirit-filled Christians to enable them to deliver those bound in sin. After conversion, Christians may need deliverance and healing ministry.

Read Acts 8:14-25

Definitions: Gifts of the Spirit

Discerning of Spirits
This gift is the miraculous power to recognize activity in the spirit realm. It is the ability to discern between the demonic and angelic forces at work in a given situation. At times it is accompanied with a "spiritual insight" into the enemy's plans and purposes.

KEY POINTS
1. Simon had apparently, according to the text, become a believer and had been water baptized.
2. Peter is used in one of the revelatory gifts of the Holy Spirit, through either Prophecy or the Word of Knowledge, or possibly the gift of Discerning of Spirits, to *"see"* into Simon's heart and to discern *"bitterness and iniquity."* Simon needed to repent and be delivered from a long-held pattern of sin. God used Peter to discern Simon's need. Simon's words also revealed his heart and his desire to continue to control others.
3. It is unclear from the text whether Simon truly breaks free from the entrenched bondage to sin, but if he sincerely repented, then we can conclude that he did.

The Christian's Need for Transformation

In the *New Spirit Filled Life Bible*, (NKJV) page 1505, the study notes to Acts 8:23 put it this way regarding The Bonds of Unforgiveness, DELIVERANCE:

> A sorcerer is one who deceives, manipulates, and delights to control others and does so by demonic enablement. Peter identified the basis for Simon's sorcery as bitterness – the deepening effects of unforgiveness (v. 2) Here is a warning regarding the danger of tolerated or embraced unforgiveness, which may, like poison, permeate and bind the soul, ultimately corrupting everything around it. In Simon's case, his bitterness shaped his passion to control others – which prompted his quest to purchase the ability to impart the gift of the Holy Spirit. Though having believed and been baptized (v. 13), the residue of his past bondage surfaces as he unworthily seeks power to manipulate others for self-exalting purposes. Peter discerns the root of his bondage (v. 23) and summons Simon to repentance and deliverance. Though Simon did not repent, this episode still points to one of the foremost keys to deliverances from entrenched bondage in a believer's soul – the act of forgiveness. Forgiving others from our heart flushes out the "poison" with the power of the Cross. In contrast, unforgiveness can, as with Simon, lead down paths we would never have imagined we would travel. (See Matthew 6:14-15; Colossians 3:13; Hebrews 12:15-17.)

According to the Hayford Bible Handbook, page 334:

> This chapter tells of a sorcerer, Simon, who had convinced the Samaritans he has some great power. Stunned by the real miracles of Peter and Philip, he professes faith and follows them to learn the secret of their power. But his old motivations are strong and he tries to buy power from Peter. Simon may have been a believer, but he was not able to share in the ministry, for his motives and character were still in the grip of sin (20-23). Salvation is for all who believe. Ministry is for those whose faith brings them significant inner transformation.

For Deeper Study
Receiving Holy Spirit fullness as a second act of grace
to empower the believer for service.

When the news of the Samaritan revival reaches Jerusalem, the apostles send Peter and John to Samaria because of their concern that *"those born of the Holy Spirit also receive the fullness of the Holy Spirit"* (New Spirit Filled Life Bible, NKJV, page 1505). Through laying on of hands and prayer by the apostles, the new believers who have previously been water baptized then receive the baptism of the Holy Spirit. (See Ephesians 4:11 about the ministerial offices for equipping the saints.)

Compare to these other passages in which the Holy Spirit is poured out:

Acts 2:1-13; Acts 8:14-17; Acts 10:44-48; Acts 19:5-6.

FOCUS POINT
God speaks to believers through the Holy Spirit and through angels and gives very specific instructions to believers who are willing to share Christ with others. He blesses their obedience and makes them fruitful Christians.

Read Acts 8:26-40

KEY NOTES
In these passages we see an example of a Spirit-led believer receiving specific guidance. God speaks directly and clearly to Philip in the following ways. Here is the summary:

1. Acts 8:26

    God sends an angel to Philip with very specific directions: "*now an angel of the Lord* <u>*spoke*</u> *to Philip* <u>*saying*</u>…"

2. Acts 8:27

    Based upon those directions, in childlike faith Philip obeys, even though the revelation is partial. God said "*go*" and Philip goes. "*...so he arose and went.*"

3. Acts 8:29

    Then the Holy Spirit speaks to Philip and tells him what to do: "*Then the Spirit* <u>*said*</u>…"

4. Philip then walks through the door God opens with the Ethiopian man in the chariot. He shares the Gospel with him in a situationally appropriate way.

5. The man is saved and baptized as a result of Philip's simple faith and obedience.

6. Compare this to John 10:27-28.

    (Jesus said) "*My sheep hear My voice, and I know them, and they follow Me. And I give them eternal life, and they shall never perish; neither shall anyone snatch them out of My hand.*"

7. Holy Spirit method of transportation: Translation

    The Holy Spirit "*caught Philip away*" (commonly referred to as translation) to another city! The Spirit of God physically moves him. The Holy Spirit moved Philip to another location. How? We don't know, but nothing is impossible with God.

For Deeper Study
My Sheep Know My Voice

Read all of John 10, especially verses 27-28. Pray and meditate on those particular verses (focus on and pray through them and ask God to bring you revelation about them). What is Jesus saying to you?

EXHORTATION
You can do it! God wants to use you.
Just as Philip preached, you can preach. Just as Philip was sensitive to the Holy Spirit, you can be sensitive to the Holy Spirit. If you are born again of the Holy Spirit through faith in Jesus, you can receive the baptism (or refilling) of the Holy Spirit to empower you for ministry, just as Philip did in Acts 8. Jesus said His disciples would hear. Philip heard and you can hear, too.

HOW CAN YOU DO IT?
Pray for the Holy Spirit to come and refill you and cultivate intimacy with Him.
Repent of any sin that is holding you back, like the bitterness and iniquity in Simon's heart. Ask Jesus, the baptizer in the Holy Spirit, to baptize you or refill you. Cultivate an intimate relationship with the Lord through spoken prayer, listening prayer, Bible reading and spending time with other believers who are hungry for more of God.

Focus Questions

1. What do Acts 6:3-7 and Acts 21:8-9 tell you about Philip?

   _____

   _____

   _____

2. What signs followed the preaching of the Gospel in Acts 8:6-8?

   _____

   _____

3. From our text, what personal characteristics of Simon show us that he is wicked?

   _____

   _____

   _____

4. What did Peter discern in Simon's heart after his conversion to Christ?

   _____

   _____

5. What did Peter urge Simon to do about it?

   _____

   _____

6. List all of the ways the Holy Spirit guided Philip in this situation.

   _____

   _____

   _____

   _____

7. What was the result?

   _____

   _____

   _____

Prayer

Lord, I pray You would reveal to me any sin in my life, particularly bitterness or unforgiveness toward others. Forgive me, I pray in Jesus' name. Please fill me afresh with your Holy Spirit.

Personal Thoughts/My Response to What I Learned

Acts 9
YOU WILL BE TOLD WHAT YOU MUST DO
Topics: The Voice of the Holy Spirit, Slain in the Spirit

Introduction

In the last session we saw the Gospel being spread to new areas because the believers were scattered through the persecution of the Church. Two of the apostles, Peter and John, went down to the revival in Samaria and affirmed what Philip was doing in evangelizing the Samaritans. The Samaritan believers were baptized with the Holy Spirit through the apostles' prayer. Miracles, healings and deliverances were happening among a people once bound in the satanic oppression of witchcraft. A sorcerer, who became a believer, was in bondage and Peter preached repentance to him. Philip, being sensitive and obedient to the Holy Spirit, heeded instructions he received from an angel to go to a certain road at a certain time. He then received further instructions directly from the Holy Spirit. Philip obeyed, and a key government official from Ethiopia was saved, resulting in opening Ethiopia to the Gospel.

We saw that the Holy Spirit has a voice and that He speaks to believers. When they are obedient to that voice, their ministry has great effect. We were also briefly introduced to Saul (later to be called Paul) in chapter 8, where we saw him consenting to the death of Stephen, the Church's first martyr. Now Saul takes center stage in chapter 9 where we see him in 9:1-2, *"breathing threats and murder against the disciples of the Lord."* He is seeking letters from the High Priest to pursue and imprison followers of "the Way" (as the church was then called) as far away as Damascus. Saul was, we will find out later in the book, a highly educated Pharisee, studied in the Jewish law. By persecuting the followers of Jesus, Saul thought he was doing God a favor until he encountered Jesus, Himself, that day on the road to Damascus.

FOCUS POINT

The effects of being in the manifest presence of God can be falling to the ground, trembling, being astonished, hearing a voice and seeing a vision.

Read Acts 9:3-9

KEY POINTS

These are the signs of the presence of Jesus on the Road to Damascus.

1. Acts 9:3

   Saul sees a bright light from heaven.

2. Acts 9:4

   A voice speaks and Saul (and his companions according to another account) falls to the ground.

3. Acts 9:6

   Saul trembles, astonished by the power of God. He recognizes the authority that is speaking to him and so when he is told *"go and you will be told what you must do,"* he does it.

4. Acts 9:8-9

    His astonishment and shock at the bright light and power of God left him in a state of blindness and fasting.

For Deeper Study
Saul's Conversion

This experience is recounted two more times in the Book of Acts. Read Acts 22:6-21, in which Paul (Saul) adds that he was later in a trance in prayer, and Acts 26:12-18.

FOCUS POINT

It was so important to God that Saul received the Holy Spirit, that He spoke directly to Ananias.

Read Acts 9:10-19

KEY POINTS

1. These are the signs of how Jesus guided Ananias in a vision.

    *   Acts 9:10

        The Lord <u>said</u> in a vision and Ananias speaks back.

    *   Acts 9:11

        The Lord <u>said</u> again. It's a two way conversation.

    *   Acts 9:12

        Ananias is <u>told</u> by the "voice" about Saul's vision, while seeing a vision himself.

    *   Acts 9:13

        Being reassured of his safety, Ananias agrees to go.

2. Acts 9:17

    The laying on of hands brings the filling of the Holy Spirit to Saul. Note that Saul had previously believed (verse 6). After he was converted, he is then baptized in water. Ananias is referred to as a *"disciple."* He prays for Saul, with laying on of hands, and Saul is filled with the Holy Spirit.

3. Ananias recognized that God is a Spirit, and that He can speak in visions. Saul came to find that out, too.

4. Read John 4:23-26, where it says God is a Spirit.

FOCUS POINT

Believers can be filled with the Holy Spirit through the laying on of hands.

Read Acts 9:20-30

KEY POINTS

1. As we saw in Acts 1:8, being filled with the Holy Spirit empowers believers to preach the Gospel.

2. Saul didn't wait around for years to begin preaching. He preached right away after being converted, filled with the Holy Spirit and baptized.

---

3. Believers today can receive the same power of the Holy Spirit to preach Christ.

FOCUS POINT
The physically dead can be physically raised through the prayer of a believer filled with the Holy Spirit.

Read Acts 9:36-43

KEY POINTS
1. Jesus tells us in Matthew 10:7-8, *"Heal the sick, raise the dead, cure the lepers and cast out demons, freely you have received, freely give."*
2. In Matthew 9:18-26 and Luke 8:51, Jesus only allowed people with strong faith to remain when he prayed for the raising of the dead.

Focus Questions
1. What are four signs that physically happened to Saul and his companions in their Damascus road encounter with Jesus?

_____

_____

_____

_____

2. Is God a Spirit?

_____

_____

3. According to John 10:3-5, should believers be able to hear His voice?

_____

_____

4. How long did Saul wait after his conversion to preach Christ?

_____

5. Based on Acts 9:40 and Matthew 9:25, what do you conclude is the role of faith when praying for the dead to be raised?

_____

_____

_____

Prayer
Father, I long to be in Your presence. I pray that You would manifest Your presence to me, and that You would speak to me. I pray that You would forgive me for the times that You have called me and I

have disobeyed. I repent of disobedience to Your call and Your voice. I pray that You would speak to me and call me, and that I would obey. God, I hunger and thirst for Your righteousness. Help me to live a victorious and obedient life in Christ. Fill me again, Holy Spirit. Thank You for Your grace. Amen.

Personal Thoughts/My Response to What I Learned

_____
_____
_____
_____
_____
_____
_____
_____
_____
_____
_____
_____
_____
_____
_____
_____
_____

Acts 10
ANGELS, VISIONS, TRANCES AND VOICES
Topics: Tongues, the Voice and Guidance of the Holy Spirit, Word of Wisdom,
Baptism of the Holy Spirit

Introduction
In Acts 9, we saw the dramatic, life-altering conversion of Saul, the killer of Christians, who became Paul, an apostle called by Jesus Christ. Saul met Jesus and encountered the manifest power of God on the road to Damascus. In his encounter with Jesus he fell to the ground, was struck blind, and was shaken to his very core. He recognized the authority of the heavenly voice that spoke to him, was converted to Christ and chose to obey. An obedient servant of the Lord, Ananias (not the man of the same name who died in Acts 5), obeyed the voice of the Lord in a vision that directed him to go pray for Saul. Through that prayer, Saul was filled with the Holy Spirit and was healed of blindness. After two threats of death against Saul were revealed, he miraculously escaped. We then saw the apostle Peter back in action when he raised Dorcas, the faithful servant of the Lord, from the dead.

In this session, we will see how the Holy Spirit divinely spoke and guided two men to meet each other and fulfill His divine purpose of extending the Gospel to the Gentiles.

FOCUS POINT
God speaks in many ways; sometimes through angels, and especially through the Holy Spirit. The Holy Spirit speaks to believers who are sensitive to Him.

Read Acts 10:1-16

KEY POINTS
1. Acts 10:2

   Notice that Cornelius is described as *"a devout man, who feared God with all his household, who gave alms generously to the people, and prayed to God always."* From this description we can conclude that Cornelius was a morally upright person, who was worshipping and obeying God to the extent of his revelation at that time. He would not have been a Jewish proselyte, but according to commentators would have been one who believed in Jewish monotheism, and ethical teachings. He needed, however, to learn the way of salvation through Jesus.

2. Acts 10:3

   Cornelius saw in a vision and the angel spoke to him. It was both a visible and an audible experience.

3. Acts 10:4

   Why was the angel sent to Cornelius? His prayers and alms had come up as a memorial before God.

4. Acts 10:5-6

   Cornelius receives instructions to send messengers to another city for a man named Simon, also called Peter, and to go to a specific address. Cornelius then quickly obeys what he hears and sees and sends the messengers to Peter in Joppa. Cornelius had faith enough to send messengers.

5. Acts 10:9-16

   Peter goes to pray and while in prayer, goes into a trance in which he hears a voice and sees a vision, the meaning of which is unclear. While wondering what it meant, three messengers show up and the Spirit of God speaks to Peter, telling him to go with them. Peter had faith enough to go.

FOCUS POINT
Prayerfulness makes believers more sensitive to the Holy Spirit.

Read Acts 10:17-33

KEY POINTS
1. Prayerfulness and a pursuit of the things of God are evident in both Cornelius' and Peter's life. They are available to the Holy Spirit. God uses those that make themselves available to Him.

2. Acts 10:19-20

   The Spirit spoke to Peter, reassuring him that the messengers were sent by God and that he should go with them.

3. Acts 10:22

   The messengers explain Cornelius' angelic encounter and the instructions he received to go and find Peter.

4. Acts 10:24-33

   Cornelius and Peter finally meet, sharing with delight and awe the divine encounters that brought them together. Both had enough faith to believe they were really hearing from God and took actions of obedience based upon what they saw and heard through supernatural revelation.

Definitions: Gifts of the Spirit

Word of Wisdom
This gift is the ability to know the right steps to take in order to accomplish the will of God. It is receiving God's divine direction for what to do and what to say in any situation or to solve any problem. It often functions in conjunction with the Word of Knowledge. The difference is, the Word of Knowledge is informational, whereas the Word of Wisdom is instructional.

Personal Application
Consider the faith that both Peter and Cornelius had to both hear and act upon Divine revelation. What specific gifts of the Holy Spirit do you think were in operation in these encounters?

FOCUS POINT
The evidence of the presence of the Holy Spirit upon the Gentiles was that they spoke in tongues, just like the Jewish believers on the Day of Pentecost.

Read Acts 10:34-48

KEY POINTS

1. Once Peter is brought to Cornelius' house, he receives understanding of the vision he had experienced.

2. Acts 10:44

   As he preaches Christ to Cornelius and his whole household, the Holy Spirit falls upon the group. God seems to have interrupted the preaching.

3. Acts 10:45-46

   The Holy Spirit falls and the Jews are astonished that Gentiles are now speaking in tongues as they had when the Holy Spirit baptized them on Pentecost in Acts 2.

4. The whole purpose of the divine encounters – the angel's visitation, the trance, the voice, and the visions – was the furtherance of the Gospel.

   - It was not to glorify Cornelius or Peter or so they could glorify themselves.
   - It was not so they could brag to their friends how God had used them.
   - It was not so they could fall on the floor and laugh at a meeting.
   - It was not so they could control and manipulate others with their "super-spiritual" behavior and put others down by building themselves up.
   - God's purpose was that His kingdom would be extended and that He would bring Himself more glory.
   - When God is good enough to speak to you in some way, thank Him, give Him glory and be humble about it.

For Deeper Study
Building Godly Character

Character is very important. Often, as Christians, we will face prolonged times of testing and trials in order for God to purify our character. Character has to be developed in us before we can truly fulfill our calling. We can cooperate with the Holy Spirit by allowing Him to help us develop the "fruit" of the Holy Spirit in our lives, including patience and long-suffering. Our character has to be able to bear up under the weight of the warfare that goes with the calling.

1. Give God alone the glory.

   Read 1 Corinthians 1:26-31, especially verse 29 which says, *"no flesh should glory in His presence."* Give the Lord glory when He uses you in a supernatural way. In other words, don't take credit or glory upon yourself.

2. Maintain a humble spirit.

   Read 1 Peter 5:5-11, especially verse 6 where Peter says to *"humble yourselves under the mighty hand of God, that He may exalt you in due time."* There are two sides of pride, which is an excessive focus on self. One is self-importance, which makes people puffed-up. Conversely, the other is low self-esteem, which can paralyze people and keep them from believing God can use them. Both are forms of pride and the way of freedom is repentance. Repenting of excessive self-focus can set one at liberty to serve Christ more effectively. Nothing is too hard for God.

Focus Questions

1. What are Cornelius' personal characteristics?

_____

_____

_____

2. Why do you think God chose Cornelius?

_____

_____

3. What did Cornelius see in a vision? What did he hear?

_____

_____

4. What was Peter doing when he heard a voice?

_____

_____

5. What happened during the trance?

_____

_____

6. What did the messengers tell Peter about why they came?

_____

_____

7. What interpretation did Peter have of the vision he received?

_____

_____

_____

8. What happened while Peter was preaching?

_____

_____

9. For what divine purpose did the Holy Spirit bring Cornelius and Peter together?

_____

_____

_____

Prayer

Father, thank You that You use ordinary people to do extraordinary things. I want to be one of those ordinary people that You use through the power of Your Holy Spirit! I praise You that You are as alive today, as You were in the Book of Acts. I pray in the name of Jesus, that You will help me to be available to be used by You. Help me to make time for prayer and reading your Word so that I know You more and can discern when You are truly speaking to me and when You are not. I want to conduct myself in a way that brings You glory. God, help me to bring more people into a saving relationship with You and bring believers to spiritual maturity. Thank You for Your answers. Amen.

Personal Thoughts/My Response to What I Learned

_____

_____

_____

_____

_____

_____

_____

_____

_____

_____

_____

_____

_____

_____

_____

_____

Acts 11
WHO WAS I THAT I COULD WITHSTAND GOD?
Topic: Remembering His Word, Office of the Prophet

Introduction

In Acts 10 we saw what could be described as a Holy Spirit inspired, supernatural phone call. Two godly, prayerful men were seeking God in different locations, and each one was supernaturally notified about the other. They were given revelation from an angel and the Holy Spirit and asked to do certain things. They believed the heavenly voices or visions they received, but they did not boast in their revelation. In fear of God, they simply obeyed. They were men of good character that God chose to use. Their obedience to the revelation they had received led to their meeting, and the result was that the Gospel was extended to the Gentiles.

When the Holy Spirit fell upon the Gentiles to whom Peter was preaching, and they received the Gift of Tongues, it was irrefutable evidence that God desired to bring them into His plan of redemption through Christ. The simple obedience of two devout people had tremendous impact to expand the Kingdom of God. From that story we saw that God, through the Holy Spirit, guides people in several ways: visions, a voice, a trance and angelic visitations. The key is that these men were seeking God, were open to being used by Him, and were obedient when He spoke. Additionally, they were not puffed up with pride about how God had used them. They were just delighted to be a part of what He was doing. They were, like Jesus, about their Father's business (Luke 2:49).

In this session, we will see Peter before the apostles in Jerusalem, defending his experience and the extension of the Gospel to the Gentiles. We will also see another very important way in which the Holy Spirit guides. He guides Christians by quickening the Word of God in their spirit and by bringing it to their remembrance. In this session, we look into key parts of the Book of John in addition to our verses in Acts 11. Students are encouraged to really dig into John 14-16 for an extended time of study.

FOCUS POINT
Obedience is required of every believer.

Read John 14-16

Jesus' parting words to His disciples are full of instructions on the relationship of a believer with the Holy Spirit. They also speak of the relationship of the three persons of the Holy Trinity; Father, Son and Holy Spirit. In these chapters, Jesus was preparing the first believers, who were to become the Church, for the outpouring of the Holy Spirit.

KEY POINTS
1. John 14:15-16, 23-24
   Obedience to the Word of God is the primary starting point to our developing intimacy with Him and discerning His leading.

- Character counts
- Obedience counts

2. It was Peter's and Cornelius' obedience to God's leading that brought the blessing upon their ministry and their lives. Ponder that thought while we look at what happened next.

FOCUS POINT
Remember the Word of God.

Read Acts 11:1-18

KEY POINTS
1. Memorizing Scripture is a key, and very important way that the Holy Spirit will speak to us and keep us from sin, as well as guide and direct us.
2. Acts 11:16
   Peter remembers the words Jesus spoke.
3. John 14:25-26
   Jesus said the Holy Spirit will *"bring to your remembrance"* things He (Jesus) had spoken.
4. In Peter's ministry in Acts 11, we see a fulfillment of just what Jesus promised before He left in bodily form. Notice the interaction of the Holy Trinity, the three-in-one God. We see Jesus promising that His Father would send the Holy Spirit. And what would the Holy Spirit do? Bring to our minds, or our remembrance, the very words that Jesus spoke. God did it for Peter as He made his case that day before the other apostles, and He will do it for you in your daily life and ministry. Peter had Jesus to speak to him in the flesh. Now we have God's written word and the Holy Spirit.

Personal Application
The importance of knowing God's written Word, along with memorizing and praying Bible verses, cannot be overemphasized. It will help us in two ways:
- It keeps us from sin or evil, especially self-deception. (See Jeremiah 17:9.)
- It helps us to discern whether what we think we are "hearing" is really the Holy Spirit, our own thoughts of the flesh, or some other spirit.

Memorize these Scriptures about God's Word: Psalm 119:11, Psalm 119:105.

FOCUS POINT:
God will help you to be obedient to His call, and He will empower you.

Read John 14:16-17

KEY POINTS
1. Jesus' words make it clear that we are not on our own in our Christian walk. In verse 16, the Holy Spirit is called the Helper, then in verse 17 He is called the Spirit of Truth. You are not intended to try in your own fleshly efforts to obey God. If that worked, we wouldn't have needed the cross or

Pentecost. We need the Word of God and the Spirit of God to help us obey God.

2. Practical application on using the Word of God.

If you are struggling with some sin and you cannot seem to overcome it, then pray to God. Ask for God's help and be diligent in your efforts to obey what He says. Find Scriptures on that topic and start to pray them out loud on a daily basis. Get a friend to pray in agreement with you regularly. You will have victory over that sin if you do not give up. At the moment of temptation in the desert in Luke 4, Jesus overcame Satan's temptations with the Word of God.

Personal Application
Help from the Holy Spirit

If you are in a situation and suddenly feel uncomfortable or convicted in your heart, or a Bible verse comes to mind, that is the Holy Spirit trying to speak to you. Don't ignore that. Listen to what He is saying. His inner prompting is not usually very loud, but His small, still voice in our spirit carries the power of God to overcome temptation. He may also be trying to protect you from danger.

Author's Note: Grow Up, Don't Blow Up!

You need both the Word of God and the Spirit of God to overcome sin and temptation. One of my favorite Bible teachers, Dr. Alan Langstaff, has a great saying:

With the Word alone, you dry up.

With the Spirit alone, you blow up.

But with the Word and the Spirit, you grow up.

FOCUS POINT

Follow the Holy Spirit where He is leading.

Read Acts 11:19-26

KEY POINTS

1. Acts 11:21

   You want to be where the Holy Spirit is leading, because that is where you will be the most productive for Christ. The phrase, *"the hand of the Lord was with them,"* indicates that the Holy Spirit was touching the hearts of the non-Jews, so they continued to preach to them and many believed.

2. Acts 11:24

   The apostles saw in Barnabas both the Gift of Faith and a man of character, which is why they chose to send him. He brought Saul to Antioch where they taught for a year, and believers were first called Christians in Antioch.

FOCUS POINT

The Office of the Prophet and the Gift of Prophecy are two different things.

Read Acts 11:27-30

For Deeper Study

There is a difference between a Christ-appointed Office of the Prophet in the New Testament and the operation of the Gift of Prophecy in the life of the believer. The *New Spirit Filled Life Bible* (NKJV), pages 1512-1513, says "predictive prophecy about specific future events was the exclusive ministry of the prophet." It also states, in part:

> "Agabus is an example of the "office" of the "prophet" in the NT. This role differs from the operation of the Gift of Prophecy in the life of the believer, for it entails a Christ-appointed ministry of a person rather than the Holy Spirit-distributed gift through a person. In the NT, this office was not sensationalized, as it tends to be today. Such an attitude is unworthy, both in the prophet and in those to whom he ministers, and is certain to result in an unfruitful end. (Apparently Paul was addressing such assumption of the prophetic office when he issued the challenge of 1 Corinthians 14:37, calling for submission to spiritual authority rather than self-serving independence.)… The office of the prophet will be characterized by preaching, teaching, miracles and renewal… The purpose of the prophetic office should be for edification, rather than entertainment – to enlarge and refresh the body, whether locally or beyond."

In the *Hayford Bible Handbook,* page 656, the Office of the Prophet as described in Ephesians 4:11 is defined as follows:

> "A spiritually mature spokesman/proclaimer with a special, divinely focused message to the church or the world. A person uniquely gifted at times with insight into future events."

The purpose of the ministry offices is to facilitate and equip the Body of the Church.

KEY POINTS

1. There is a difference between a Christ-appointed Office of the Prophet in the New Testament and the operation of the Gift of Prophecy in the life of the believer.
2. Move under God's direction, not your own initiative.
   - Avoid presumption and doing things God did not call you to do.
   - As American Bible teacher Joyce Meyer says, don't covet someone else's position in ministry, unless you are willing to suffer what they've suffered.
   - Do not promote yourself in ministry. If you're asked to do a job because someone in leadership recognized a gift in you, do that job with a humble heart, but don't strive for power or position. Those who humble themselves will be exalted in due time. There is a waiting time and a preparation time in ministry.
   - God knows where you are in your own spiritual development. If you try to promote yourself, you will not be able to withstand the spiritual warfare at that higher level. God resists the proud, but gives grace to the humble.
   - Don't compare yourself to others, just ask God to help you be the best you that you can be.

- Wait on God and trust His timing. Serve Him with a grateful heart and continue to pray for your leaders.

Focus Questions

1. Review Peter's and Cornelius' experience in Acts 10 as summarized in Acts 11. Would you say they were obedient to the supernatural revelation they received?

_____

2. Based on John 14:15 and John 14:23-24, what does Jesus say about obedience?

_____
_____

3. What promise did Jesus make to believers in John 14:25-26?

_____
_____

4. How do you see that promise fulfilled in Acts 11:16?

_____
_____

5. List and memorize the two names that Jesus uses for the Holy Spirit in John 14:16-17. What does this say to you?

_____
_____
_____

6. What does Jeremiah 17:9-10 say about your heart and your ability to deceive yourself?

_____
_____
_____

7. What does the above verse, in conjunction with Proverbs 11:14, indicate about having other believers speak into your life?

_____
_____
_____

8. What was the result of Agabus' prophecy about a coming famine in Acts 11:28?

_____
_____
_____

Prayer: Help me Lord!

Lord, I need Your help! I pray that You would help me to have a desire to read Your Word and that when I do, You would help me to understand it. Apart from You I can do nothing, so please help me Lord! Help me to obey Your Word, to keep myself from sin, and to overcome habit patterns, thought patterns and speech patterns that are sinful in my life. Help me not to view or to read things that are sinful. I ask You to keep me from self-deception and to help me to discern Your leading and guidance in my life. Help me to serve You and others in humility. I pray that You will reveal Your plans and purposes for my life more clearly, and help me to complete those purposes. I pray for godly wisdom and counsel from believers who are more spiritually mature than I am. Help me to have the grace and patience to wait for the fulfillment of Your specific callings and promises to me. I love You, Lord, and I want to obey You, so please help me! Amen.

Personal Thoughts/My Response to What I Learned

Acts 12
THE POWER OF PRAYER TO OPEN PRISON DOORS
Topics: Angelic Visitation, Prayer

Introduction
In Acts 11, we saw Peter describing the way the Holy Spirit spoke to him and brought him together with Cornelius for God's purposes. The result was the Gospel being spread to the Gentiles. Simple faith and radical obedience brought about great results. We saw that obedience to God's leading and good, moral character are key components to being used by God. We also saw that one of the ways that the Holy Spirit communicates with believers is by bringing Scripture to mind. The words of Jesus in John 14 assure us that He (through the person of the Holy Spirit) will bring His words to our mind. This serves to both keep us from sin by convicting our conscience, and to confirm the Holy Spirit's leading through God's Word. Next we see that persecution once again comes to the Church, and that powerful prayer spares lives and opens prison doors.

FOCUS POINT
Following Jesus Christ does not mean that we will not suffer, or even lose our lives, for our faith.

Read Acts 12:1-4

KEY POINTS
1. Acts 12:2

   James was killed because he was a Christian. This James was the brother of John, not the half-brother of Jesus who became the head of the Church at Jerusalem. James became the first of the 12 apostles to be martyred.
2. Peter is seized and thrown in jail.

   Herod was evil and seeking popularity by killing Christians. The following verses describe what happens to counteract that evil.

FOCUS POINT
Intercessory prayer is powerful and in response, God releases angels to do His bidding on our behalf.

Read Acts 12:5-19

KEY POINTS
1. Acts 12:5

   Constant prayer was being offered on his behalf.
2. Acts 12:7

   The arrival of the angel is a direct result of the "constant prayer" offered to God by the church.
3. There is power in intercessory prayer, which is defined simply as prayer offered on behalf of another. See definition of intercession (following).

For Deeper Study
Intercessory Prayer/Intercessor

Read the following Scriptures regarding intercession.

- Isaiah 53:12
- Romans 8:26
- Hebrews 7:25
- James 5:16-18

Here are the definitions of *intercession* and *intercede* from Webster's Dictionary.

> **Intercession** *(noun)*
> 1. the act of interceding
> 2. prayer, petition, or entreaty in favor of another
>
> **Intercede** *(intransitive verb)*
> 1. to intervene between parties with a view to reconciling differences
> 2. to mediate

FOCUS POINT
God sometimes uses holy angels to communicate with and deliver believers from peril.

KEY POINT
1. Acts 12:9
   Even though Peter did not understand that what was happening to him was real (he thought it was a vision), the angel of the Lord appeared to him and brought him out of the prison.
2. The angel was physically manifested before Peter. He struck Peter on the side while he was sleeping.
3. The presence of the Lord's angel caused the chains to fall off Peter's wrists.
4. Compare to Daniel 3:25. *"Look!" he answered. "I see four men loose, walking in the midst of the fire; and they are not hurt, and the form of the fourth is like the Son of God."* In both cases, an angel removed chains from bound believers and brought them out of captivity.
5. The angel had a voice and spoke directly to Peter and gave him instructions. The angel obviously understood the peril that Peter was in, and urges him to hurry.
6. The angel disappears and Peter comes to himself. He realizes that what happened to him was not a dream, but happened in the physical realm and that he really was set free.
7. The believers in the prayer meeting were surprised when Peter showed up at the door as a result of their prayers. They, too, didn't realize at first that Peter was really physically present with them.

FOCUS POINT
In the end, God brings justice.

Read Acts 12:20-24

KEY POINTS

1. God, in His sovereignty, allowed James to die. When the church prayed fervently on behalf of Peter, Peter was delivered from the prison. Perhaps the prayerlessness of the church, contributed to James' death. It is hard to say.

2. This text demonstrates the danger of self-glorification. Herod didn't recognize that it was almighty God who gave him his position of authority, so when he took glory upon himself, the Lord sent an angel of the Lord to strike and kill him.

3. Acts 12:24

   The result of persecution countered with intercessory prayer is that *"the word of God grew and multiplied."*

Focus Questions

1. Who harassed the church, killed James and imprisoned Peter?

   _____

2. What do you think Peter was feeling? Do you think he was comfortable?

   _____

   _____

3. What happened in verse 5?

   _____

   _____

   _____

4. What do you think is the relationship between verse 5 and verse 7?

   _____

   _____

   _____

5. What does the angel say and do to Peter?

   _____

   _____

   _____

6. Is this a physical experience for Peter or just a vision?

   _____

7. Although God allowed James' death at the hands of Herod, in the end, where did James end up after his death?

   _____

   _____

Prayer

God, I thank You that You are with me during times of suffering and persecution for my faith. I thank You that You bore my pain, and carried my sorrows upon Your body as it was nailed to the cross for my sins. I pray that You would come, by Your Holy Spirit, and minister to me during difficult times. Lord, I ask for Your help to walk in freedom from self-pity and selfishness, two of the tools that the enemy of my soul tries to wield against me to get me to give up my faith. I pray and I repent of walking in self-pity, and of any self-centeredness that is in my heart. I thank You for freedom, and I thank You for a deep understanding to come to me of how You identify with me in my times of suffering. Thank You that I am never alone. Help me to grow stronger in faith during those times and to press in to more prayer and more of seeking You, just like the Church did on Peter's behalf. I ask in Jesus' name, that You would anoint me by Your Holy Spirit's power to pray, not only for myself, but for others who are suffering and for the Church. I pray for the gift of intercession, as Your Holy Spirit wills. I thank You that the weapons of our spiritual warfare are not fleshly or carnal, but that they are mighty in You for the tearing down of strongholds, those thought patterns and mindsets that are not pleasing to You. Father, break strongholds off of my mind that I could walk in liberty, wielding the weapon of prayer with great authority and with great effect.

Personal Thoughts/My Response to What I Learned

Acts 13
AS THEY MINISTERED TO THE LORD AND FASTED
Topics: The Voice of the Holy Spirit, Fasting, Office of the Pastor/Teacher,
Discerning of Spirits

Introduction
In Acts 12 we saw James being put to death for his faith. Then the Church prayed fervently on behalf of Peter, who had also been jailed for his faith, asking that his life be spared. God brought about Peter's miraculous rescue from prison through an angelic visitation. We saw that intercessory prayer releases God's power through holy angels. God sometimes uses angels to communicate with and rescue believers in peril. In the end, we saw Herod reaping the reward of his wickedness. His death resulted from his own pride. So, God avenged James' death at the hands of Herod. In Acts 13, we will see another important aspect of prayer through revelation about the power of prayer and fasting. In addition, we will receive an important admonition about sorcery. Remember that the focus of our study is on how God provides leading and guidance to believers, and we will see another example of that in this session.

FOCUS POINT
Corporate fasting and prayer can make us more sensitive to the Holy Spirit. It is one way to help us discern God's will.

Read Acts 13:1-3

KEY POINTS
1. Acts 13:1
    Two of the four (or five, as some count them) church leadership offices are mentioned; the Office of Pastor/Teacher and the Office of Prophet.

For Deeper Study

While some in the Body of Christ treat the two ministerial offices of Pastor and Teacher (listed in Ephesians 4:11) separately, the *Hayford Bible Handbook,* page 656, defines them as one as follows:

> "The word *pastor* comes from a root meaning "to protect,' from which we get
> the word *shepherd*. Implies the function of a shepherd/leader is to nurture,
> teach, and care for the spiritual needs of the body."

Those who define Pastor and Teacher separately refer to the five-fold ministry offices, but those whose view is that Pastor/Teacher is one office refer to the four-fold offices.

---

2. Acts 13:2
    A time of corporate prayer and fasting led to the choice of Saul and Barnabas for missionary work.

3. Definition: ministered (Strong's #3008)

    leitourgeo (lie-toorg-eh-oh)

    Performing religious or charitable acts, fulfilling an office, discharging a function, officiating as a priest, serving God with prayers and fastings. (Compare "liturgy" and "liturgical") The word describes the Aaronic priesthood ministering Levitical services (Hebrews 10:11). In Romans 15:27, it is used of meeting financial needs of the Christians, performing a service to the Lord by doing so. Here the Christians at Antioch were fulfilling an office and discharging a normal function by ministering to the Lord in fastings and prayer. (From the *New Spirit Filled Life Bible*, NKJV, page 1515.)

4. Notice that during a time of fasting and prayer, the Holy Spirit *"said."* That indicates that the Holy Spirit has a voice, and that He speaks and that He gives specific directions to believers who are corporately fasting and praying and ministering before Him.

5. Fasting should be a regular spiritual discipline for Christians.

6. Fasting is an act of personal sacrifice before the Lord, and helps one to grow spiritually stronger as the flesh is weakened. There are several types of fasts in Scripture. There are partial-day fasts, such as Peter fasting and praying in Acts 10:9-10. (Peter fasted and prayed on the rooftop before lunch and then received the vision that brought about the extension of the Gospel to the Gentiles.) Also, there are multiple-day fasts, as in Jesus' fast in the wilderness. Jesus said, *when* you fast, not *if* you fast (Matthew 6:16). Fasting can be cleansing for body and spirit, and should be part of the normal Christian life.

Author's Note

I find if I fast an evening, then wake up early the next morning to pray, I am more easily convicted by the Holy Spirit so I can repent and be cleansed. I was trained to fast regularly in Bible school, and it is something I practice at least one meal or one day per week. Then there also are times when I am called to fast on a three-, seven- or ten-day basis for special purposes, sometimes even a 21- or 40-day partial fast.

For Deeper Study
Other Scriptures on fasting

Luke 4:1-13: Jesus fasted 40 days in the wilderness and resisted temptation with the Word of God after being baptized, but prior to entering into public ministry.

Matthew 6:16-18: Jesus gave instruction on fasting.

Daniel 10:2-6: A 21-day partial fast brings angelic response.

FOCUS POINT

The empowerment of the Holy Spirit for ministry can come through a leader's impartation.

KEY POINTS

1. Acts 13:2-3

The Holy Spirit spoke and called certain men to a certain task during a time of fasting and prayer, and then impartation of the anointing was transferred to them through the laying on of hands.

2. Read Romans 1:11

   Paul spoke of imparting spiritual gifts.

3. Acts 13:4

   They were sent out, not by men, but by the Holy Spirit.

4. Look at all that follows in the rest of the chapter as a *result* of that time of fasting and prayer. Paul gets discernment about a sorcerer, and preaches a mighty sermon to a hostile crowd.

FOCUS POINT

One of the gifts of the Holy Spirit is known as the Discerning of Spirits.

Read Acts 13:9-10

KEY POINTS

1. Read also 1 Corinthians 12:7-11, especially verse 10 regarding the gift of the Discerning of Spirits. When Paul *"looked at him intently,"* the Holy Spirit showed him something and Paul received spiritual revelation about the man in that moment.

2. According to Stevan Williamson in his book, *Who's Afraid of the Holy Ghost?* (page 137), this gift can be defined this way:

   The discerning of spirits is supernatural revelation by God which allows a person to see the presence, activity and intent of a spirit. This includes a revelation regarding the type of spiritual activity that is motivating a particular person. Discerning of spirits includes both Godly and evil spirits. It also includes a discerning of human spirits, whether evil or good in their intentions.

3. Note that scripturally there is no gift of discernment, it is called the gift of Discerning of Spirits. A separate gift of the Holy Spirit is called the Word of Knowledge. We'll discuss the Word of Knowledge further in relation to Acts 14.

4. Paul makes a declaration about the man according to the spiritual revelation he received. Notice the text states that *"Paul, filled with the Holy Spirit, looked intently at him and said..."* Paul is not worried about what the evil man or anyone else thinks of him. He is not politically correct. Paul calls evil, evil. Paul cursed the sorcerer and he was struck blind through the Holy Spirit. Coming against God's work had terrible consequences for the sorcerer.

5. Compare the way popular American culture accepts and glorifies witchcraft and sorcery (e.g. books and movies, such as Harry Potter, Wizards of Waverly Place, Bewitched, etc.) and what the Bible says in Deuteronomy 18:9-11:

   "When you come into the land which the LORD your God is giving you, you shall not learn to follow the abominations of those nations. There shall not be found among you anyone who makes his son or his daughter pass through the fire, or one who practices witchcraft, or a soothsayer, or one who interprets omens, or a sorcerer, or one who conjures spells, or a medium, or a spiritist, or one who calls up the dead.

Personal Application

Compare the acceptance of such materials in modern, Western culture (including among some people in the Church) to Acts 19:18-20.

For Deeper Study
Other Scriptures on the Discerning of Spirits

Acts 8:18-23: Simon the Soothsayer.
Acts 16:16-18: Paul and the soothsaying woman.

Focus Questions

1. What were the disciples doing at the time they received revelation?

   _____

   _____

2. What happened as the result of what they were doing?

   _____

   _____

3. Does the Holy Spirit have a voice?

   _____

4. What did they do in verse 3?

   _____

   _____

5. Who sent out Saul and Barnabas?

   _____

6. What happens in the rest of the chapter as a result of the fasting and prayer in the first few verses? Is that ministry productive?

   _____

   _____

   _____

7. When Paul looked at the sorcerer, what did the Holy Spirit show him about that man? (See also 1 Corinthians 12:7-11 about the Discerning of Spirits.)

   _____

   _____

   _____

8. What does Paul say to the sorcerer? Does he accept sorcery as being an alternative theology or does Paul, filled with the Holy Spirit, call evil, evil?

_____

_____

_____

9. Based upon the above passages, do you think a Christian should view or read witchcraft-themed material?

_____

_____

_____

Prayer

Lord, I pray that You would help me to discipline my flesh to fast, pray, and minister before You. Help me to do this, not for the attention of people, but so that I may overcome my flesh and be strengthened in my spirit and draw closer to You. I pray that I would know You more and more, and be sensitive to Your voice. I pray that I would have revelation to know Your Word and know Your voice. I pray for the ability to discern good from evil and truth from false teaching. I pray that You would reveal to me the desires of Your heart, and the ministry that You have set me apart for. Thank You for Your Word. Thank You for Your Spirit. Thank You that You love me. Amen. So be it.

Personal Thoughts/My Response to What I Learned

_____

_____

_____

_____

_____

_____

_____

_____

_____

_____

_____

_____

_____

_____

_____

Acts 14
SEEING THAT HE HAD FAITH TO BE HEALED
Topics: Word of Knowledge, Faith, Healings and Miracles

Introduction

In Acts 13 we saw the power of fasting and prayer to help the disciples discern God's will and make them sensitive to hear the Holy Spirit's voice. The Holy Spirit spoke and Paul and Barnabas were anointed for the work to which God had called them. They received impartation of the anointing through the laying on of hands by the Apostles and were sent out.

This was Paul's first missionary journey and it is detailed in Acts 13 and 14. They encountered opposition to their ministry from unbelieving Jews, as well as a sorcerer. Paul called the sorcerer and his works evil. Paul cursed the sorcerer and the sorcerer was struck blind. This sign caused an important man, a proconsul in that town, to come to faith in Jesus Christ.

Paul was bold in the Lord. He was not politically correct. Paul and Barnabas did not call witchcraft just another "alternative" religion, they spoke the truth boldly and the truth, followed by the sign of the sorcerer's blindness, set a captive man free.

In this session, we see this missionary journey continue and watch the Gospel go forth. Paul speaks the truth boldly again, despite great opposition. Remember that our focus in this study relates to how the Holy Spirit guides us and communicates with us. In this chapter we look at how He guided Paul.

FOCUS POINT
Sensitivity and obedience to the Holy Spirit are keys to fruit-bearing ministry.

Read Acts 14:1-10

KEY POINTS
1. Acts 14:9-10
   Paul "saw" that the man had faith to be healed.
2. He did not "see" this with his natural eyes, but through spiritual revelation.
   This is a manifestation of the spiritual gift of the Word of Knowledge, then the healing took place through the Gift of Healings.
3. Compare to the passage in Acts 3:4-10.
   Here Peter notices something about the lame man, just as Paul "sees" that a man has faith to be healed. Both Peter and Paul, two believers out in public, were sensitive to, and obedient to the Holy Spirit's inner promptings.
4. As mentioned previously in the discussion of Acts 11, obedience to the Holy Spirit's leading is a key to developing spiritual intimacy with the Holy Spirit. This is discussed frequently in John 14-16, chapters that provide a great deal of wisdom for believers. In these chapters, Jesus taught about the Holy Spirit while preparing his followers for his crucifixion. He wanted them to know He would not be leaving them alone, but that He would send the Holy Spirit.

For Deeper Study
What did Jesus say about the Holy Spirit and believers?

- Believers will do greater works than He did (John 14:12).
- The Helper (Holy Spirit) will teach believers all things (John 14:26).
- The Holy Spirit will declare to believers what God says (John 16:13).

FOCUS POINT
The gifts of the Holy Spirit are available to all believers.

Read 1 Corinthians 12:1-11

KEY POINTS
1. Discuss the gifts of the Holy Spirit, especially the gift of the Word of Knowledge.
2. Author Stevan F. Williamson in his book, *Who's Afraid Of The Holy Ghost?*, describes the Word of Knowledge as follows: "The gift of the word of knowledge is the supernatural revealing by God to an individual of certain facts relating to people, places, events and/or situations. This gift relates to either the present or the past. It is by supernatural revelation, not related to a person's intelligence."
3. In addition to Paul's Word of Knowledge, the lame man had faith to be healed. It is probable that this was the Gift of Faith given by the Holy Spirit in that moment.

Definitions: Gifts of the Spirit

Gift of Faith
This is the supernatural ability to believe and trust God completely, without doubt in His words and His faithfulness, no matter what kind of circumstances a person is facing. The Gift of Faith is a grace of the Holy Spirit that is beyond the faith that brings salvation.

---

4. The Holy Spirit gives gifts as He wills.
   You can ask, but it is up to the Holy Spirit to give. The only way you will know if you have received it is to start exercising your gifts.
5. Prayer + Bible Reading = A Believer who is Sensitive to the Spirit
   Developing an intimate relationship with the Holy Spirit through personal prayer and devotional Bible reading makes believers more sensitive to the Holy Spirit in public situations. In Jesus' ministry, as well as in Peter and Paul's, revelation gifts and miracles usually followed personal or corporate prayer.

For Deeper Study
Other biblical examples of the Word of Knowledge can be found in the following passages:
- The story of Jesus and the Samaritan woman in John 4:16-18.
- Peter and Cornelius in Acts 10:1-6, 19-20.

FOCUS POINT
When God isn't done with you, even death cannot stop you when praying disciples surround you!

Read Acts 14:11-20

KEY POINTS
1. Paul calls it like he sees it. He calls useless idols useless. He also refuses to receive the pagans' worship when the Holy Spirit uses him in a miracle.
2. For all his efforts, Paul is stoned, left for dead and is miraculously raised from the dead after stoning. Paul had not yet fulfilled his destiny in Christ. The prayers of the Spirit-filled disciples were used to raise Paul through the operation of the Working of Miracles.

FOCUS POINT
Nothing stops the furtherance of the Gospel.

Read Acts 14:21-28

KEY POINTS
1. The Gospel continues to go forward despite the persecution.
2. The church is expanded, many are converted, and disciples are strengthened in faith.
3. Acts 14:22

    Paul says to his disciples, *"We must through many tribulations enter the kingdom of God."* God did not promise us a problem-free life, but He will deliver His children and bring them through difficulty.

Focus Questions
1. Using the gift list in 1 Corinthians 12:8-10, which other gift or gifts, besides the Word of Knowledge, do you think Paul was operating in? What about the lame man?

    _____

    _____

2. Who gives the gifts?

    _____

3. Why are the gifts given?

    _____

4. Comparing Acts 14:9-10 to Acts 3:4, do you notice a similarity between these experiences of Peter and Paul when they encountered a sick man?

    _____

    _____

    _____

5. Focusing on verse 20, what power was there in the disciples who surrounded Paul? In what gift did they operate?

_____

_____

6. Reading what Paul says in verse 22, what does this say to you about your own life and walk with Christ?

_____

_____

_____

_____

7. Compare verse 22 to 2 Thessalonians 1:3-8. What do these verses say to you about Christian suffering?

_____

_____

_____

_____

Prayer

Lord, help me to walk in the fullness of the Gospel. I ask You to show me my personal mission, purpose and destiny in life, and to fill me afresh with Your Holy Spirit so that I may fulfill it. Cleanse my heart, make my motives pure, and use me I pray, in Jesus' name. I pray also that You would help me in times of suffering, not to be weak in faith or filled with fear. I pray that I, like Paul, would get up and keep moving forward after I am knocked down. I pray for perseverance in faith and hope in You. I pray all these things in the mighty name of Jesus Christ. Amen.

Personal Thoughts/My Response to What I Learned

_____

_____

_____

_____

_____

_____

_____

_____

_____

_____

_____

_____

Acts 15
IT SEEMED GOOD TO THE HOLY SPIRIT AND TO US
Topic: *Wisdom in the Counsel of Elders, Office of the Apostle*

Introduction
In Acts 14, we saw Paul and Barnabas continuing their missionary journey, Paul's first, through the cities in Asia Minor. They had been sent out from the Church in Antioch after a time of fasting and prayer with the prophets and teachers. The Holy Spirit had spoken, setting them apart for their specific work, and they had received impartation through the laying on of hands and had gone out.

Preaching first in the synagogues and then in the marketplace, they encountered much opposition to their preaching. The Holy Spirit's power was evident in their ministry, as signs and wonders accompanied their preaching, and many Gentiles were converted. We saw them being used in the gifts of Discerning of Spirits, the Word of Knowledge and Healing, among others. The power of God flowing through them confirmed that the Holy Spirit was with them.

Returning to Antioch at the end of the missions trip, they stayed there on furlough, reporting all that God had done through them. It was there in the Church at Antioch, while Paul and Barnabas were resting at their home base, that a conflict arose. Certain men came preaching another Gospel.

FOCUS POINT
Godly dispute resolution includes submission to godly authority.

Read Acts 15:1-12

KEY POINTS
1. In Acts 15:2-7, we see that a dispute has arisen in the Church. In order to understand the dispute, it's necessary to remember that the Gospel is spreading from a mono-cultural, all Jewish group of people, to a multi-cultural situation in which Gentiles of various ethnicities are becoming believers. Some of the Messianic-Jewish believers are having trouble separating themselves from the requirements of the Old Testament law.
2. A group referred to as "the Judaizers" begins to oppose Paul's preaching that faith alone, by God's grace, is enough for salvation. At issue is the pivotal Christian doctrine known as "justification by faith." They try to make the Gentile converts to Christ obey certain aspects of the Jewish law found in the Old Testament.
3. They are, in effect, legalists, trying to put additional rules and regulations on top of the Gospel and thereby rob people of their freedom in Christ. For example, they were saying that to be saved, it is not enough to believe in Jesus Christ as your savior, you also had to practice circumcision, obey Jewish food laws, and more.
4. This was a very, very important early theological issue – Paul's revelation of salvation by grace alone, through faith, is being challenged.

5. Paul is arguing that if one is saved by faith alone, that one will also grow into Christian maturity through that same faith and by the Holy Spirit's work in their lives, rather than by obedience to rules and regulations.

For Deeper Study
Galatians 2:11-21; 3:1-9

In order to fully understand the dispute in Acts 15, it should be read in conjunction with the Book of Galatians, which Paul wrote to the group of churches in that region around the same time. In Galatians, Paul first establishes his apostolic authority and then emphasizes the point that one is saved by faith alone, rather than by works of the law (e.g., males being circumcised or keeping food laws according to the Old Covenant).

Office of the Apostle Defined

According to *The Hayford Bible Handbook,* page 656: In apostolic days, the title *apostle* "referred to a select group chosen to carry out directly the ministry of Christ; included the assigned task given to a few to complete the sacred canon of the Holy Scriptures. Implies the exercise of a distinct representative role of broader leadership given by Christ. Functions as a messenger or spokesman of God. In contemporary times refers to those who have the spirit of apostleship in remarkably extending the work of the church, opening fields to the gospel, and overseeing larger sections of the body of Jesus Christ."

---

6. The dispute is so great that Paul, Barnabas and those with whom they had this dispute, went up to Jerusalem to discuss the question with the apostles and elders there. There was a sharp theological schism, and they knew they needed wise counsel.

7. Sometimes disagreements in church are so severe that we must submit ourselves to the authority of leaders to help us work them out. This is particularly true where matters of scriptural interpretation are in question.

FOCUS POINT
Godly dispute resolution includes submission to the guidance of the Holy Spirit.

Read Acts 15:13-35

KEY POINTS
1. In Acts 15, we see godly, sincere, believing people, who disagree with each other, working out their dispute in accordance with the guidance of the Holy Spirit.

2. Acts 15:28

   The apostles said, *"it seemed good to the Holy Spirit and to us,"* as they issued their decision. The guidance of the Holy Spirit came through a corporate meeting with the elders and the apostles of the church. This is an example of the wisdom found in Proverbs 11:14, *"Where there is no counsel, the people fall; But in the multitude of counselors there is safety."*

3. Even the great Apostle Paul, hand picked by Jesus, knew that the nature of the dispute was so great that he and Barnabas needed the wisdom of the elders at Jerusalem. Christianity is not a "solo" occupation, but there is safety in wise counsel and at times, seeking good advice of other believers who are more mature.

4. James issues the Jerusalem Decree, and Paul and Barnabas deliver the letter containing the resolution to the conflict, to the church in Antioch.

5. There is evidence of much liberty in the church in Antioch, as they received the letter with joy, and *"it seemed good"* for some to stay there preaching and teaching.

6. In verse 32 Judas and Silas, *"themselves being prophets also exhorted and strengthened the brethren with many words."*

FOCUS POINT
Sometimes "agreeing to disagree" and parting ways, resolves our disputes.

Read Acts 15:36-41

KEY POINTS
1. Sometime later, after preaching back at their home base for a while, Paul and Barnabas could not agree on whether to take John Mark with them on their next missions trip. John Mark had abandoned the first trip, and apparently Paul felt him to be disloyal or unreliable.

2. The contention between them became *"very sharp"* and Paul and Barnabas parted company.

3. God can bring good out of any situation.
   Note that now, instead of one missionary team, God has two:
   - Barnabas goes out with John Mark.
   - Paul goes out with Silas.

The Moravian Church motto puts it best:
"In essentials unity, in non-essentials liberty, and in all things love."

Focus Questions
1. What do Galatians 2:20-3:3 mean to you personally, both about your salvation and about spiritual growth in Christ?

_____

_____

_____

_____

_____

2. How does spiritual growth and maturity come, according to Paul?

_____

_____

_____

3. Can you "earn" or be "good enough" by your works, to earn salvation?

    _____

4. Should we work out disputes on our own, or should we submit ourselves to the authority of more mature Christian leaders to help us work them out?

    _____

    _____

    _____

5. In what setting did the guidance of the Holy Spirit come?

    _____

    _____

6. What was the response of the church in Antioch when the apostles (in a meeting known as the Jerusalem Council) issued their decision?

    _____

    _____

7. Read Proverbs 11:14. What does this verse say to you about seeking godly advice?

    _____

    _____

8. Read Matthew 18:15-17. What are the steps to take when there is a dispute or an offense between two believers?

    _____

    _____

    _____

    _____

9. How did Paul and Silas resolve their conflict?

    _____

    _____

    _____

Prayer

God help me to seek Your guidance in those areas of my Christian walk in which I disagree with other believers. Help me to be humble and to submit to godly authority that You have placed in my life. I thank You that I am not saved by my own works or any goodness of my own, but by Your sacrificial death for me, out of Your love. Help me not to place rules or bondages upon myself that are beyond what You call me to, but to walk in the liberty and freedom for which You have set me free. You said in Your Word that it is for "freedom that You have set me free!" Thank You for that knowledge. Where I disagree with brothers and sisters in Christ, help me to seek Your guidance and the wise counsel of mature believers. Where necessary, help me to "agree to disagree" and part ways if it would lead to greater peace and the furtherance of the Gospel. Help me to be loving, kind and free in Christ, and help me to grant that same freedom and liberty to those around me. Amen!

Personal Thoughts/My Response to What I Learned

Acts 16
THEY WERE FORBIDDEN TO PREACH THE WORD IN ASIA
Topics: Holy Spirit Guidance, Deliverance, Discerning of Spirits

Introduction

In Acts 15, we saw two examples of resolving disagreements between Christians. When some of the Jewish believers had tried to require Gentile Christian converts to follow Old Testament laws, a dispute arose that was so important to the spread of Christianity, that Paul and Barnabas and those with whom they disagreed, took the matter before James and the elders in Jerusalem for resolution. The doctrine of justification by faith was at issue, and they submitted the question to their apostolic leaders in Jerusalem to resolve the matter. We saw from this example, that God sometimes leads and guides us through the wise counsel of more mature Christians, and that wisdom comes from the guidance received through group prayer and submission to godly authority.

Later in the chapter, we saw Paul and Barnabas disagreeing on a less crucial matter (whether to include John Mark on the next missions trip), and their dispute being so sharp that they parted ways. Despite the disagreement and separation of Paul and Barnabas, the Gospel went forward, now with two teams being sent out instead of one. Barnabas went out with John Mark, and Paul went out with Silas. No disagreement among believers will stand in the way of the furtherance of God's purposes.

In this session, we see Paul and Silas begin Paul's second missionary journey. We pick up the story with Paul and Silas going up into Syria from Jerusalem, strengthening the churches there and meeting a young believer named Timothy, who joins them. The second missionary journey is covered in Acts 16-18. Acts 16 provides ample opportunity for us to see how the Holy Spirit guides, so let's begin by studying Paul's second missionary journey.

FOCUS POINT

The guidance of the Holy Spirit can be both "negative" (prohibiting certain actions) and "positive" (encouraging certain actions).

Read Acts 16:1-10

KEY POINTS

1. Acts 16:6

   The text says they *"were forbidden by the Holy Spirit,"* but does not tell us how the Holy Spirit communicated it. Some possible ways could have been:
   - Inner promptings
   - Prophetic utterances by a believer
   - External circumstances

2. Acts 16:7

   Here again it says the *"Spirit did not permit them."* One way the Holy Spirit could have forbade them from going to Asia can be found in 2 Corinthians 2:13, where Paul states, *"I had no rest in my spirit..."*

3. Acts 16:9

When Paul had a night vision, he and Silas concluded that they were being called to Macedonia.

4. Acts 16:10

They *"immediately"* looked for a way to get to Macedonia. Once they were sure of the Spirit's guidance, they left without delay! In other words, they obeyed God.

5. Summary of the Holy Spirit's guidance in Acts 16:1-10.

   - *No!* He "forbids" and shuts the door to two locations (negative/prohibiting).
   - *Yes!* He gives vision and opens the door to another location (positive/directing).
   - Continued guidance and ministry success came when they were *obedient* to the last thing He prompted them to do.

For Deeper Study
The Guidance of the Holy Spirit

Negative Guidance

- In Acts 16:6-7, we see the Holy Spirit "forbidding" or "disallowing" as a way He guides.
- See also 2 Corinthians 2:13, where Paul had *"no rest in his spirit."*

Positive Guidance

- Visions are one way the Holy Spirit guides believers, as in Acts 16:9.
- Read Acts 10:9-16 for an example of another vision.
- Read and meditate upon Proverbs 3:5-7.
- This is a conditional promise. What conditions must you meet in order for God to *"direct your path"?*

Compare Acts 16:6-7 to 1 Thessalonians 2:18.

   One time the Holy Spirit is *"forbidding"* the missionaries from going to Asia minor and instead sending them to Macedonia, and the other time the disciples recognized that *"Satan hindered us."*

It is sometimes difficult to tell if the Holy Spirit is forbidding us or if we are being opposed by Satan. When in doubt, pray and wait for God's answer.

Author's Note: Once guidance is confirmed, obedience should be quick.

An important part of being sensitive to the Holy Spirit's promptings and leadings is obedience. A wise woman once taught me a little phrase for my kids to remember: "I OBEY, RIGHT AWAY." The same goes for believers. If you are obedient in the small things He prompts you to do, He'll give you more to do.

FOCUS POINT

Ministry that is guided by the Holy Spirit is fruitful.

Read Acts 16:11-15

KEY POINTS

1. Paul and Silas see immediate fruit from their ministry in the conversion of Lydia, an important saleswoman in that region. She and her whole household are saved and baptized. Lydia was most likely a single woman of means, who was a merchant and was likely a continuing financial supporter of Paul throughout his ministry.

2. Lydia displays the gift of hospitality immediately after her conversion to Christ, inviting the apostles to stay at her house.

For Deeper Study
The Church at Philippi

The Book of Philippians reveals Paul's continuing relationship with the Church at Philippi which was established on his second missionary journey. He writes from a Roman jail to his beloved church on the topic of joy. Read Philippians for a deeper word on walking in joy no matter the circumstances.

FOCUS POINT

The gift of Discerning of Spirits, along with the believer's authority in Christ, can bring freedom to demon-possessed people.

Read Acts 16:16-24

KEY POINTS

1. Acts 16:16-18

   This girl was *"possessed with a spirit of divination,"* and went about telling fortunes. Notice that what she was saying was true, but Paul was able to discern the ungodly spirit behind her words. This is a clear example of the gift of the Discerning of Spirits. Compare this to the story of Elymas the sorcerer in Acts 13:9-12.

2. A list of the gifts of the Holy Spirit, including the Discerning of Spirits, is found in 1 Corinthians 12:4-11.

FOCUS POINT

Praising God during bad circumstances can bring miraculous freedom.

Read Acts 16:25-40

KEY POINTS

1. Paul and Silas had been whipped and jailed for their faith, nevertheless they were praising God, singing hymns at midnight.

2. Some of the fruit of the Macedonian mission came in the jailhouse through the conversion of the jailer.

3. Note that later, writing from a Roman prison to the church in Philippi, Paul commands, *"Rejoice in the Lord always"* (Philippians 4:4). Paul knew what he was talking about.

For Deeper Study
Finding the good in bad circumstances

Notice that despite their imprisonment, Paul and Silas chose to praise God. Their praises seem, in this account, to have a cause and effect relationship with their sudden, miraculous freedom. Whatever the case, we can make the same choice; to praise God in spite of our circumstantial comfort (or lack of comfort). Our attitude will change for the better, whether or not we see immediate results.

Read Romans 8:18-39.

Romans 8:27-28 carries a promise we should all remember. *"Now He who searches the hearts knows what the mind of the Spirit is, because He makes intercession for the saints according to the will of God. And we know that ALL things work together for good to those who love God, to those who are called according to his purpose."*

Personal Reflection: Compare your reactions to bad circumstances to that of Paul and Silas. The next time you face difficulty, ask God for His grace to praise Him no matter what.

Focus Questions

1. Find three ways that the Holy Spirit guided the missionaries.

   _____

   _____

   _____

2. How is this an example of Proverbs 3:5-7?

   _____

   _____

3. Once it became clear that they were to go to Macedonia, did Paul and Silas waste any time?

   _____

4. What was the first "fruit" of Paul & Silas' obedience?

   _____

5. Based on the Acts 16 accounts of the possessed woman's deliverance and Lydia's conversion, do you think women are important to God?

   _____

   _____

6. What did Lydia do after her conversion?

   _____

   _____

7. What did the spirit of divination allow the slave girl to do?

_____

_____

_____

8. What spiritual gift did Paul display in this passage and in Acts 13:9-12? (Hint: See 1 Corinthians 12:4-11.)

_____

9. How do you think the praises of Paul and Silas affected their situation?

_____

_____

Prayer

Father, thank You that Your Holy Spirit guides believers today, just as You did during Paul's lifetime. Lord, help me to be more sensitive to Your guidance and to be obedient to Your promptings. I pray that You would cleanse my heart and forgive me of doubt, unbelief, and for those times when I have disobeyed You and not listened to Your voice. I pray that I would trust in You with all my heart and lean not on my own understanding, in all my ways acknowledging You, and that You would direct my paths. I further pray, in Jesus name, that You would help me to have vision like Paul, and to praise You in the "prison" (very difficult) circumstances of my life. I pray that I could be more like Lydia, who opened her heart to the Gospel spoken by Paul, and then opened her home to Christians in hospitality. I pray that You would help me to know that ALL things work together for the good of those who love God and who are called according to Your purposes. Thank You for making me a fruitful Christian. Amen!

Personal Thoughts/My Response to What I Learned

_____

_____

_____

_____

_____

_____

_____

_____

_____

_____

_____

_____

Acts 17
AND SOME OF THEM WERE PERSUADED
Topic: Holy Spirit-Directed Ministry

Introduction
After the split with John Mark, Paul and Silas had set out upon their second missionary journey. As we saw in Acts 16, twice they tried to go into various parts of Asia, but they were forbidden or prohibited by the Holy Spirit from going there. The text is unclear as to how the Holy Spirit did this, only that He did. Finally, we saw Paul getting very clear, direct guidance from the Holy Spirit in the form of a night vision of a man calling him to come to Macedonia.

Following the leading of the Holy Spirit through the vision, they set off for Macedonia. First they ministered at Philippi, saw the conversion of Lydia and her household and established a church. After a power encounter in which a demon-possessed fortune-teller was delivered from an evil spirit, they were beaten with rods and jailed. Immediate opposition from the enemy camp had risen up against them after the successful conversion of Lydia. Nevertheless, they did not shrink back from their God-ordained mission, even in the appalling conditions of a Philippian jail.

With wounds still fresh from the beating they received for the sake of their preaching, they did not lose hope. Praising God at midnight, a miraculous earthquake occurred that loosened the chains of the prisoners and opened the jail doors. An opportunity is given for the conversion of their Philippian jailer, and he, along with his whole household, is saved through faith in Jesus Christ. Like Lydia, the jailer opened his home to Paul and Silas after his conversion to Christ and nursed their wounds. In Chapter 17, we see the disciples continue in their mission to Macedonia.

FOCUS POINT
Continue in the last thing you know the Holy Spirit called you to, until you receive clear direction or fresh calling.

Read Acts 17:1-15

KEY POINTS
1. Acts 17:1-2
   Paul continued in the ministry for which God ordained him.
2. The importance of perseverance in God.
   Continue doing the last thing you are certain He called you to do, until you are released or redirected.
3. Read Luke 18:1-8 (persisting in prayer) and compare Paul's persistence in his mission to Jesus' instructions to persist in prayer.

For Deeper Study

Women have played an important role in the Church since the very beginning.

In Acts 17:4, 12 and 34, Luke specifically notes the conversion of important or prominent women, indicating the important role women played in the establishment of the Church.

Compare to the story of Lydia's conversion in Acts 16:11-15.

Paul greets various women in his letters, such as in Romans 16:1-16 where we see the mention of Phoebe and Julia.

FOCUS POINT

Holy Spirit directed ministry is fruitful ministry, whether you are called to sow the seed, water the crops, or reap a harvest.

Read Acts 17:16-34

KEY POINTS

1. Compare Acts 17:4 (where a "great multitude" joined Paul and Silas) and Acts 17:32-34 (where "some mocked" and "some men joined"). We see that great multitudes in Macedonia believed, but there was less fruit in the ministry among the super-intellectual, idol worshippers in Greece.
2. What we know is that Paul received a very specific, clear call to Macedonia (Philippi, Thessalonica and Berea) through the vision and that ministry was very fruitful
3. Note that there are later epistles or letters written by Paul to the Churches he had founded on this missionary journey (Philippians, First and Second Thessalonians), but no such letter to "Athenians."
4. It may be an oversimplification, but it can reasonably be argued that where God was clearly directing Paul, his ministry was more fruitful. We do not know why he went to Greece, except that he was escaping for his life. However, Paul perseveres and preaches the Gospel despite the resistance of the Athenians. Paul was given an immediate harvest in Macedonia, but he was also faithful to sow seed in Athens when the opportunity presented itself.
5. The guidance of the Holy Spirit, the invisible hand of God, kept Paul from being killed in Berea and helped him escape, so he could later write the epistles. Obviously, God's hand was upon Paul

---

Personal Application

Read Proverbs 3:5-10, which reads in part, *"Trust in the Lord with all your heart, lean not on your own understanding, in all your ways acknowledge Him and He will direct your path."* Make this your personal prayer.

Focus Questions

1. Read Luke 18:1-8. What does this passage say to you about continuing in prayer?

_____

_____

---

2. How did Paul show persistence in his mission?

     _____

     _____

3. In looking at the Scriptures above, what is God's view of women in the Church?

     _____

     _____

4. Compare Acts 17:4 to 17:32-34. What was the difference in the result of the ministry at Macedonia versus Athens?

     _____

     _____

     _____

Prayer

Lord, guide me. Help me daily to seek Your guidance and direction through Your Word, through prayer, through listening for Your voice, and by recognizing Your hand in my life through circumstantial guidance. I need Your help, God. I pray that, like Paul, I will be joyful in all circumstances, knowing that You love me, and that You are good. I pray that You would bind the enemy, and the powers of darkness that hinder my walk with You, and that You would loose the Holy Spirit in my life. I pray that Your Kingdom will come and Your will is what will be done in my life. Help me to do the acts of the Holy Spirit – healing the sick, binding up the broken hearted, delivering the oppressed and preaching Your Word with boldness, in the Church and in the marketplace, by the power of Your Holy Spirit. In Jesus' name. Amen

Personal Thoughts/My Response to What I Learned

_____

_____

_____

_____

_____

_____

_____

_____

_____

_____

_____

_____

_____

_____

_____

_____

Acts 18
NOW THE LORD SPOKE TO PAUL IN THE NIGHT
Topics: Night Visions, Compulsion to Testify

Introduction
In Acts 16, we saw Paul receiving a clear call to Macedonia in a night vision, and throughout that chapter and Acts 17, we saw the fruit of Paul's ministry there. Many multitudes of Greeks and prominent women became believers during the Macedonian mission. Then Paul traveled to Athens, having barely escaped from an angry mob of unbelieving Jews. He preached in Athens among the intellectuals and saw little fruit from his ministry in a city given over to idols. Nevertheless, Paul did not quit. He continued on and moved next to Corinth. In Acts 18 we will see that he again received very clear direction from the Lord.

FOCUS POINT
The Holy Spirit compels believers to testify that Jesus is the Christ. We must choose to obey that prompting in order to be a witness.

Read Acts 18:1-8

KEY POINTS
1. Acts 18:3

   Paul taught on the Sabbath in the synagogue, but he had a "day job" too. He was a tentmaker. Rabbis in ancient Judaism were not allowed to be paid for their teaching.
2. Acts 18:5

   Here it tells us that Paul was *compelled* by the Spirit and *testified* of Christ to the Jews.
3. The compulsion of the Holy Spirit came so that Paul would *testify* that Jesus is the Christ. This is an example of what the Word tells us in Acts 1:8, "*You shall receive power when the Holy Spirit comes upon you, to be my WITNESSES.*"

For Deeper Study
Compelled by the Holy Spirit

Compelled is the same word as used in 2 Corinthians 5:14 – *sunecho* (soon-ekh-oh) Strong's #4912. From *sun* (together), and *echo* (to hold); hence, "to hold together" or "to grip tightly."

The word describes people who are afflicted with various diseases and pains (Luke 4:38) or paralyzed by fear (Luke 8:37); crowds hemming Christ in (Luke 8:45); an army surrounding Jerusalem (Luke 19:43); soldiers arresting Jesus and holding Him fast (Luke 22:63).

In every use of the word, there is a sense of constraint, a tight grip that prevents an escape. The love of Christ leaves us no choice except to live our lives for Him.

From the *New Spirit Filled Life Bible,* NKJV, page 1616.

FOCUS POINT
The guidance of God may come in a night vision and in a reassuring voice.

Read Acts 18:9-17

KEY POINTS
1. Acts 18:9

   Paul received a night vision from the Lord in which He spoke to him and he was reassured of his safety and urged to continue in his preaching in Corinth. A dream would be while Paul was asleep, but this was apparently a night vision, presumably while Paul was awake.
2. Paul took God at His word, obeyed Him, and then stayed another year and a half in Corinth.
3. The clear guidance of God came through a night vision here and in Acts 16:9 (the Macedonian call). God fulfilled His word to Paul in both cases.

FOCUS POINT
God often uses other believers to guide us in our walk with Him.

Read Acts 18:24-28

KEY POINTS
1. Apollos was a believer and teacher, but knew only the baptism of John (water baptism for repentance and public declaration of faith). He may have been teaching that the Messiah was yet to come and (according to Jack Hayford's commentary) Aquila and Priscilla may have shared Christ with him.
2. God used Aquila and Priscilla to instruct him more fully on the Holy Spirit. They took Apollos aside rather than publicly correcting him, displaying both humility and wisdom.
3. This will become important in Acts 19 as Paul goes to Ephesus.

Focus Questions
1. What was Paul's occupation?

   _____

2. Who did God send to work alongside Paul?

   _____

3. What was Paul "compelled" to do by the Holy Spirit?

   _____

4. Looking back in Acts 1:8, what is the purpose for which the Holy Spirit is given?

   _____

   _____

5. In Acts 18:9, how did the Lord speak to Paul?

    _____

    _____

6. Personal Reflection: Consider a time when you received clear guidance from the Lord. Write a brief testimony of that experience.

    _____

    _____

    _____

    _____

    _____

    _____

    _____

    _____

    _____

    _____

    _____

    _____

    _____

Prayer

Lord, I pray that in the same way that You guided Paul and his missionary team, that You would guide me. Help me to receive the power of Your Holy Spirit so that I can testify of You, both in Church and in the marketplace as Paul did. I pray that You would speak, lead and guide me. Thank You for pouring out Your Holy Spirit upon me and giving me the power to be Your witness! Amen.

Personal Thoughts/My Response to What I Learned

_____

_____

_____

_____

_____

_____

_____

_____

_____

_____

_____

_____

_____

_____

_____

Acts 19
GOD WORKED UNUSUAL MIRACLES BY PAUL'S HANDS
Topics: Miracles, Transferring the Anointing, Baptism of the Holy Spirit

Introduction
In Acts 18, we saw the guidance of the Lord coming in both a *"compulsion"* to preach the Word of God, and through a night vision. The voice of the Lord had spoken to Paul during the night vision, reassuring him that he should continue preaching in Corinth, and that he would be protected there. God led and kept Paul safe in his ministry. God also guided Paul to connect with like-minded believers (Aquila and Priscilla, a couple who had a house church) in his profession of tentmaking in order to receive economic provision. They were tentmakers by day, preachers on the Sabbath and by night. In this session, we see the third missionary journey of Paul continue as he preaches and revisits churches that he previously planted. We'll look again at the role and guidance of the Holy Spirit in Paul's ministry. Paul's third trip took him back to Galatia, to Ephesus for two years, to Greece and to Macedonia. He wrote the two letters to the Corinthians, as well as the Book of Romans during this period.

FOCUS POINT
The Baptism of the Holy Spirit is for believers and it empowers them to be a bold witness for Christ.

Read Acts 19:1-10

KEY POINTS
1. Acts 19:1-2

   Here we see Paul encountering *disciples*, which indicates that they were born again believers. Yet he asks them a question that seems a little unusual: *"Did you receive the Holy Spirit when you believed?"* Something about them, or an inner prompting, must have come to Paul to make him address them in this way. (Compare to Acts 8:14-17.)

2. This echoes Acts 18:24-28 where Apollos knew only the baptism of John (water baptism for the remission of sins), and had to be instructed by Aquila and Priscilla about Jesus and the coming of the Holy Spirit. Perhaps the disciples here had been previously instructed by Apollos and didn't understand the finished work of Jesus and the Holy Spirit as poured out on the Church at Pentecost. It is also possible that Paul had previously encountered Apollos' disciples.

3. Acts 19:5-6

   Paul had to further explain the Gospel to them, and then he laid hands on them so they could receive the fullness of the Holy Spirit.

4. When the Holy Spirit came upon them, they did two things: they *spoke in tongues* and *prophesied.* (Compare to Acts 2:4, and Acts 10:44.)

5. Acts 19:7

   In addition to the Gift of Tongues and Gift of Prophecy, further evidence that the Holy Spirit had come upon the believers was that they were very bold witnesses.

FOCUS POINT
You have to know Jesus before you can use His name.

Read Acts 19:11-20

KEY POINTS
1. Acts 19:11-12

   Signs accompanied Paul's ministry. Through Paul's hands, and even through articles of his clothing, diseases left people and evil spirits went out of them.

2. Compare this to Peter's shadow healing someone as he passed by in Acts 5:15. This is a sign that an invisible, but tangible presence of the Holy Spirit manifests through believers who have been filled with the Holy Spirit. It can remain upon their clothing and go out from their presence too.

3. According to study notes in the *New Spirit Filled Life Bible* (NKJV), page 1499, "sometimes God uses physical objects as a point at which our faith may make a kind of link between the seen and the unseen. The bread and cup of Communion, the water of baptism, and the anointing oil of James, are all such points of contact."

4. Jesus says in Luke 8:46, in the healing of the woman with the issue of blood, "*Somebody touched Me, for I perceived power going out from Me.*" That power is the anointing or manifest presence and power of the Holy Spirit.

5. Acts 19:14-16

   Those without faith in Jesus Christ, who try to cast out demons using the name of Jesus, open themselves up to attack from the demonic powers.

6. Using Jesus' name is not magic. It's use is reserved for believers in Jesus Christ who have put their full faith and trust in Him, being born again by grace, through faith.

For Deeper Study
The Anointing/The Manifest Power of God

The invisible, but real, power of the Holy Spirit that manifests in healing, deliverance, signs and wonders through believers in Jesus Christ is often referred to as "the anointing." Some additional Scriptures to read, in which the anointing of the Holy Spirit brings miraculous results, are:

- 2 Kings 6-7 (The miraculous floating ax head.)
- Isaiah 10:27 (The anointing breaks the yoke.)
- Acts 5:15 (Healing through Peter's shadow.)
- Luke 8:40-56 (Jesus perceived power going out from Him.)
- 1 John 2:20-27 (The anointing teaches all things.)

Each of these are an example of what the anointing of the Holy Spirit does, or a description of the anointing and its effects.

FOCUS POINT

Successful ministry can arouse spiritual warfare.

Read Acts 19:21-41

KEY POINTS

1. The move of God through Paul's ministry once again incurs backlash from the unbelievers, and spiritual warfare breaks out following his successful ministry. We see a very dramatic example of this in the riot at Ephesus. The idol makers became angry that Paul was preaching against idol worship and stirred up a mob against Paul. The demonic powers behind the idolaters tried to stir the crowd against Paul. Notice that verse 32 indicates the *"confusion"* of the crowd. Demonic activity creates confusion. Paul was protected through the intervention of people who encouraged him not to enter the theatre.

2. Nevertheless, the Gospel moves forward and Paul is once again kept safe by the Lord for His purposes.

A Personal Challenge

Do you need a fresh outpouring of the Holy Spirit? Perhaps you should consider having a pastoral or apostolic leader lay hands on you and pray for you to receive a fresh anointing of the Holy Spirit, too!

Focus Questions

1. Whom did Paul encounter as he came through Ephesus?

_____

2. What question did Paul ask them?

_____

3. What happened after these disciples were re-baptized in water, and then the apostle laid his hands upon them?

_____

_____

4. What experience is common in Acts 2:4, Acts 10:44-48 and Acts 19:5-6?

_____

_____

5. What two things happened through Paul's hands, and even through articles of his clothing in Acts 19:11-12?

_____

_____

6. In Mark 16:14-18, what five signs did Jesus say would follow those who believe?

_____

_____

_____

7. What happened to the unbelievers who tried to use the name of Jesus to exorcise a demon when they didn't know Jesus by faith?

_____

_____

8. Personal Reflection: Consider Acts 19:5-6, 19:11-12, and Mark 16:17-18 and what this says to you as a believer. Are you experiencing this yet in your walk with Jesus? If not, how do you think you can begin to experience these things?

_____

_____

_____

_____

_____

9. How could the scene in Ephesus be described as being motivated by spiritual warfare (the invisible battle between Satan's demonic spirits and God's holy angels) played out in an earthly scene?

_____

_____

_____

_____

_____

Prayer

Father, revive me that I might walk in the fullness of Your Holy Spirit's power and be all that You have purposed for me to be. Bring revival to me and to Your Church. God, bring the fear of the Lord and an awakening to me and to Your Church worldwide. Lord, we are desperate for Your Holy Spirit. Holy Spirit, come. Bring a healing revival, dear God. Do it in accordance with Your will and in the name of Your blessed Son, Jesus Christ, so that many will come to know You and be saved, I pray. Amen!

Personal Thoughts/My Response to What I Learned

_____

_____

_____

_____

_____

Acts 20 & 21
THE HOLY SPIRIT TESTIFIES THAT CHAINS AWAIT PAUL

Topics: Raising the Dead, Inner Witness of the Spirit, Prophetic Declarations, Office of the Evangelist

Introduction

In Acts 19, we saw believers receive the Baptism in the Holy Spirit through Paul's prayer. They spoke in tongues and prophesied. They were also empowered to be witnesses. In Paul's ministry, the sick were healed, the demon-possessed were delivered and many were led to faith in Jesus Christ. In this session, we see a man raised from the dead, and Paul receives several prophetic warnings of coming difficulty. Despite this, he presses on in his God-given mission.

FOCUS POINT

The dead can be raised by the power of the Holy Spirit working through believers.

Read Acts 20:7-12

KEY POINTS

1. As Paul was preaching a late night revival meeting, a young man fell asleep, fell out of a window and died. Paul rushed to his side, and in a clear demonstration of the Holy Spirit's power, raised the young man from the dead.
2. This is a continuation of what Jesus began in his earthly ministry, and showed that the church was continuing to move forward.
3. This is another demonstration of the gifts of the Spirit as found in 1 Corinthians 12:1-11. It is also a demonstration of Jesus' command to *"heal the sick, raise the dead, cleanse the lepers, cast out demons"* in Matthew 10:8.

FOCUS POINT

Prophetic warnings can prepare believers for coming difficulty.

Read Acts 20:17-38

KEY POINTS

1. Paul clearly felt he was to go to Jerusalem.
   We see that in Acts 19:21 when Paul *"purposed in the Spirit"* to go, as well as in Acts 20:22-24 when Paul felt he was *"bound in the spirit"* to go to Jerusalem.
2. Acts 20:38
   Just as clearly, Paul's friends did not want him to go, and *"they sorrowed because they would see his face no more."*
3. Acts 20:23
   Paul had apparently been previously notified by the Holy Spirit on more than one occasion that he

would be chained and imprisoned in Jerusalem.

4. We do not know whether the Holy Spirit communicated these things to Paul through inner promptings of the still small voice of the Spirit, or through several prophetic utterances, but we'll see a demonstration of this in Acts 21.

Read Acts 21:1-14, 26-36

KEY POINTS

1. Here we see a progression of people delivering warnings to Paul; Paul remaining determined to go to Jerusalem; and finally the prophetic warnings being fulfilled.

2. Acts 21:4

    Disciples *"told Paul through the Spirit"* that he shouldn't go to Jerusalem.

3. Acts 21:8-9

    In Caesarea the team *"entered the house of Philip the evangelist...(who) had four virgin daughters who prophesied."* Philip is mentioned as holding the Office of the Evangelist. This was the same Philip who had led the Ethiopian government official to the Lord in Acts 8:26-40. Also, note that his daughters prophesy, a continuing fulfillment of Joel 2 that says *"your sons and your daughters shall prophesy."*

Office of the Evangelist Defined

According to *The Hayford Bible Handbook,* page 656, the Office of the Evangelist "refers primarily to a special gift of preaching or witnessing in a way that brings unbelievers into the experience of salvation. Functionally, the gift of evangelist operates for the establishment of new works, while pastors and teachers follow up to organize and sustain. Essentially, the gift of evangelist operates to establish converts and to gather them spiritually and literally into the Body of Christ."

---

4. Acts 21:10-11

    A prophet named Agabus showed Paul what would happen to him. He prophetically demonstrated the word of the Lord. Apparently, Agabus held the Ephesians 4:11 Office of the Prophet. This gave him more leeway in exercising the gifts than the believer who is limited to *"edification, exhortation, and comfort"* as described in 1 Corinthians 14:3.

5. Acts 21:12

    Paul's friends *"pleaded with him not to go."*

6. Acts 21:14

    Paul *"could not be persuaded"* and they left for Jerusalem.

7. Acts 21:32-33

    Paul is finally bound in chains at Jerusalem, fulfilling the prophetic warnings he had received. At the time, this actually saves Paul's life and gives him a chance to preach, which we will see in Acts 22.

For Deeper Study
Personal prophecies and what to do with them.

The study notes for Acts 21:4-12 in the *New Spirit Filled Life Bible* (NKJV), page 1530, say:

Note that the passage contains several warnings given by the Spirit that Paul would encounter trouble during his visit to Jerusalem. But the apostle persisted, later being arrested and sent to Rome under guard. Arguments as to whether or not Paul was in the perfect will of God are pointless. What is useful to note:

1. Personal prophecy does not have to dictate the decisions or manipulate the will of a godly person and

2. Even though they may be true, God's purpose may yet be realized, as was the case in God's will ultimately bringing Paul to Rome.

According to the *New Spirit Filled Life Bible* (NKJV), page 1531 (in part), believers should remember to consider the following factors when evaluating possible "words from God" through other people:

1. Acts 20:22-24

   The word is not "new" to the mind of the hearer, usually it is something they've been dealt with by God about or He has already begun to reveal it to them, as was the case with Paul here.

2. Acts 11:28; 21:10

   Weigh the character of the person with the word. Here, Agabus had a track record.

3. Christian prophecy is not "controlling."

   Paul did not change his plans based upon that word, but he could prepare himself and he could have people praying for him.

4. Luke 2:19

   Never respond hastily to a prophetic word. Wait upon the Lord, weigh it and hang onto it like Mary did.

5. The operation of the Gift of Prophecy is different than an Ephesians 4:11 Office of the Prophet type of operation. (Agabus is an example of someone in the Office of a Prophet.) Remember that the primary purpose of the prophetic gift in the New Testament is three-fold according to 1 Corinthians 14:3:

   - Exhortation – to stir up (believers in their faith and to obedience)
   - Edification - to build up (the Body of Christ in His service)
   - Comfort (Encouragement) - to cheer up (encourage believers)

6. Say it or Pray it?

   When given an impression from the Lord for another person, ask the Holy Spirit before speaking. Weigh it, hang onto it, and put it to the 1 Corinthians 14:3 test. Often you are to "pray it and not say it." Weigh whether it is a prophetic word or an intercessory prayer burden.

8. To say that the people prophesying Paul's chains at Jerusalem were in sin would be too strong and not supported by the text. However, they may have been adding their own feelings (Don't go, Paul. We're going to miss you.) to what the Holy Spirit was telling them. As it turned out, their prophecies were true. It is also possible that the Holy Spirit was using the prophecies to get a whole group of people praying for Paul, and psychologically preparing him for being taken into custody in Jerusalem. We will see Paul going to Rome in chains as we press on in the Book of Acts, and in that prison, much of our New Testament was written.

For Deeper Study
Read the story from the life of Jesus in Matthew 16:13-23

Compare this to revelations Paul was receiving and the reactions of the people.

Peter had just declared Jesus as the Christ by the revelation of the Holy Spirit. In the next paragraph, Jesus calls Peter *"Satan"* for trying to dissuade Him from going on His God-given mission to Jerusalem. One minute Peter got it right, walking by the Holy Spirit, and the next minute, operating by a different spirit, he sins and ends up tempting Jesus not to obey God and go to the cross. Peter was clearly rebuked by Jesus as he was in sin.

Focus Questions

1. What spiritual gifts do you think were in operation when Paul raised a man from the dead?

   _____

   _____

   _____

2. What Ephesians 4:11 ministry office did Philip hold? What does the text say about his daughters?

   _____

   _____

3. What did all the prophetic words warn Paul about if he went to Jerusalem?

   _____

   _____

4. What was Paul's response?

   _____

   _____

5. Personal Reflection: Have you ever received confirmation through an accurate prophetic word from another person? Write a brief personal testimony that you can share with someone.

   _____

   _____

   _____

Prayer

Lord, I want to hear Your voice. Please help me to discern Your guidance and help me to obey Your will. Lord, would You confirm things that I am hearing in my spirit, through other trustworthy believers, with prophetic utterances, and through Your Word? Please use me to be sensitive to Your voice so that I will pray for others as You are prompting. Also, use me to give exhorting, edifying and comforting words to other believers. I pray that in all these things I would operate in love. In Jesus' name I pray. Amen.

Personal Thoughts/My Response to What I Learned

_____

_____

_____

_____

_____

_____

_____

_____

_____

_____

_____

_____

_____

_____

_____

_____

Acts 22
A GREAT LIGHT SHONE AND PAUL FELL TO THE GROUND
Topics: Slain by the Holy Spirit, Visions

Introduction

In Acts 20 and 21, we saw Paul raising a dead man, preaching the Gospel in Ephesus, escaping from a mob, and receiving several prophetic warnings from the Holy Spirit and through a variety of people, that he would face chains in Jerusalem. Nevertheless, Paul continued on to Jerusalem where we see the prophetic words come true, as Paul is taken into custody. It is worth noting that, through prophetic words, Paul was prepared for the difficulty he would face for preaching Christ. God's guidance did not mean Paul would be comfortable, but it was, no doubt, reassuring. While in chains, Paul requests permission from his captors to address the crowd. We see Paul beginning his defense before the Jews while in custody in Jerusalem at the beginning of Acts 22. Paul shares his personal testimony of conversion to Christ and supernatural encounter with Jesus as a significant part of his speech. Paul's chains were an opportunity to preach the gospel.

FOCUS POINT

The presence of God can have a visible and audible manifestation.

Read Acts 22:1-21

KEY POINTS

1. Jesus guided and manifested Himself to Paul in several ways in these passages.
2. Acts 22:6

   There was a **visible** manifestation when Paul says, *"a great light shone around me."*
3. Acts 22:7

   There was an **audible** manifestation as Paul says he *"heard a voice speaking to me."*
4. Acts 22:7

   Paul had a **physical** reaction to the presence of God as he *"fell to the ground."*
5. There are two other accounts of Paul's conversion experience, in Acts 9:1-19 and Acts 26:12-18. Reading the accounts together gives a fuller understanding of the experience Paul had. The three accounts of Paul's conversion are pivotal in the Book of Acts and worthy of deeper study.
6. Paul's conversion experience also demonstrates to us the effect a powerful encounter with God can have on people.
7. Here is a summary of the manifestations of God's presence in Acts 22:
   - Verse 6: Visible – *"a great light from heaven shone around me."*
   - Verse 7: Physical falling – *"I fell to the ground"*
   - Verse 7: Audible – *"I heard a voice"*
   - Verse 9: Fear of God – *"saw the light and were afraid"*
   - Verse 11: Struck blind – *"I could not see for the glory of that light"*

- Verse 13: Divine healing through prayer – *"receive your sight"*
- Verse 14: Prophecy – *"God has chosen you"*
- Verse 17: Trance during prayer – *"I was in a trance"*
- Verse 18: Audible direction – *"get out of Jerusalem"*

FOCUS POINT

The presence of God can physically weaken the flesh of man, causing him to fall to the ground.

For Deeper Study
Falling to the ground in His holy presence

One thing that happened to Paul is that he *"fell to the ground."* In the church, we commonly refer to this as being slain by the Holy Spirit. Look up these passages for other instances of people who were unable to stand in the presence of the Lord.

- Abram in God's presence: Genesis 17:3, 17
- Israelites when fire came down from heaven: Leviticus 9:23-24
- Moses & Aaron in the presence of the glory: Numbers 20:5-7
- Ezekiel in the presence of the glory: Ezekiel 43:3; 44:4
- Daniel in response to a vision: Daniel 8:17
- Peter, James and John on the Mount of Transfiguration: Matthew 17:5-7
- The guards about to arrest Jesus in Gethsemane: John 18:4-6
- Leper imploring Jesus to heal him: Luke 5:12
- John and the 24 elders in Christ's presence: Revelation 1:17; 5:8

FOCUS POINT

During times of deep prayer, a believer may go into a trance and God can speak to him.

KEY POINTS

1. A disciple named Ananias, having been notified by the Lord through a vision and a voice, goes to Saul, heals his blind eyes through laying his hands on him, and prophesies over Saul.
2. Notice that after he leaves Ananias, Paul goes to the temple to pray, goes into a trance and sees a vision and hears the voice of the Lord warning him to leave.
3. Another example of a believer, in prayer, going into a trance is Peter in Acts 10:10-13.
4. During their respective trances, both Peter and Paul heard the Lord speak in an understandable voice.

FOCUS POINT

In the midst of chaotic circumstances, God's advance warning and Divine providence can protect obedient believers.

Read Acts 22:22-30

KEY POINTS

1. The Jewish crowd turned on Paul as he preached that God had sent him to the Gentiles.
2. God divinely protected Paul during the chaos.
3. Paul also used his knowledge of Roman law to protect himself.
4. The prophetic warnings given in Acts 20-21 about Paul's impending captivity in Jerusalem came true here.

Focus Questions

Read and compare the three accounts of Paul's conversion found in the following passages: Acts 22:6-21, Acts 9:1-19, Acts 26:12-18.

1. In what ways did Jesus manifest His presence in Paul's conversion?

_____

_____

_____

_____

_____

2. Was there a time when you were overwhelmed with the Lord's presence in a very tangible, physical way? Briefly explain the situation in a short personal testimony if you have one.

_____

_____

_____

_____

_____

_____

_____

3. Compare Acts 10:10-13 and Acts 11:5 with Acts 22:17-21 What happened to both Peter and Paul while they fell into a trance during prayer?

_____

_____

_____

4. How did God sovereignly protect Paul from the angry mob?

_____

_____

_____

5. Looking back at Acts 21:10-11, did that prophecy by Agabus come true?

_____

_____

6. How did God use Paul's natural knowledge to keep him safe when in the Roman barracks?

_____

_____

_____

Prayer

Lord, I need Your presence. Father, I pray that You would draw me into a deeper intimacy with You. Give me the ability to read Your Word consistently, to pray and to listen for Your voice. Keep me tender toward You that I could repent if I sin against You. Lord, draw me near to You and bring me back to my first love, the Lord Jesus Christ. Overwhelm me with Your love and manifest Your holy, glorious presence again, in Jesus' name. Amen.

Personal Thoughts/My Response to What I Learned

_____

_____

_____

_____

_____

_____

_____

_____

_____

_____

_____

_____

_____

_____

_____

_____

Acts 23 & 24
THE LORD STOOD BY PAUL
Topics: Night Visions, the Voice of the Holy Spirit, Divine Providence

Introduction

In Acts 22 we saw Paul, in chains, recounting his conversion through a power encounter in which he saw a glorious light, heard a voice and was felled to the ground in the presence of the Lord. This is one of three major accounts of Paul's conversion in the Book of Acts. It details the various manifestations that Paul experienced as he saw a vision of Jesus on the Damascus Road. As a result, he was converted from a killer of Christians to a follower of Jesus Christ.

Paul, recounting this experience and his Jewish heritage, gives his defense before the crowd in Jerusalem. Paul's preaching while in custody is a fulfillment of prophetic words that had previously come to him. The Holy Spirit had warned him of impending imprisonment in several ways. When the crowd became hostile towards Paul as he preached, God used his Roman captors to protect him from the mob. Then Paul, through his knowledge of Roman law, asserts his Roman citizenship to avoid scourging. We now find Paul under Roman guard, standing before the council of the High Priest of the Jews in Jerusalem, for clarification of the charges being brought against him.

FOCUS POINT
God uses night visions and His presence as ways to communicate with believers.

Read Acts 23:1-11

KEY POINTS
1. Paul used his knowledge of the differences between the Sadducees and Pharisees (political factions) to his advantage by bringing disagreement between them and dividing his enemies.
2. The Sadducees did not believe in the supernatural power of God, the resurrection of the dead, angels, demons, etc. (That's why they were "sad, you see."), but the Pharisees did.
3. Once again, Jesus stood by Paul and spoke to him.
4. This seems different than what Paul had experienced before when he was having a night vision. (For examples, see Acts 16:9 and 18:9-11.) The plain meaning of the text—*the Lord stood by him*—should be taken literally.
5. Here we see the Lord speaking to Paul and telling him that he would not only testify at Jerusalem (where he was currently imprisoned) but also that he would go on to Rome. That would have given Paul a great deal of comfort. Paul had learned that he could take God at his Word.
6. The word was also a confirmation of earlier prophetic words Paul had received about his captivity and journey to Rome.
7. In other words, Paul knew he wasn't going to die while imprisoned in Jerusalem, which should have been cause for Paul to simply relax, despite his current, very uncomfortable and, no doubt frightening, circumstance.

FOCUS POINT
God can use seemingly bad circumstances for our good and His glory.

Read Acts 23:16-35, Acts 24

KEY POINTS
1. Divine providence is reflected in the guidance of the Holy Spirit.
    In Acts 23:16, God uses Paul's nephew to uncover a plot against Paul, which ultimately leads to the Romans taking Paul back into custody and protecting him in the barracks. In that way, God used the chains of the Romans to protect Paul and spare his life.
2. According to *Harper-Collins' Bible Dictionary*, pages 890-891, providence is defined, in part, "as one of the most commonly held and most vigorously debated beliefs in both ancient and modern times: that there is a benevolent and purposeful ordering of all events of history. Nothing happens by chance; though not always perceptible to human understanding, there is a divine or cosmic plan to the universe, a reason for everything. The communities of faith reflected in the documents of the Bible also held a view of providence. In contrast to pagan or fatalistic worldviews, God the Creator was held to be personally responsible for preserving and regulating the created order. In this context, providence is related to notions of "election" and "predestination." This God has a plan for his world. Providence is not a principle or reason; rather providence is the will of the Creator who is actively involved in moving his creation to a goal."

For Deeper Study
Peace in the midst of difficulty

Sometimes it is difficult for us to see it at the time, but as was the case with Paul, what seem to be "chains" in our life (either literally or figuratively in the form of difficult circumstances) can actually be used by God to protect us. Paul had previously received words of his impending imprisonment, so was no doubt comforted that God was present, even in his chains. So it is with us. As we are prepared for difficulty by God's Word, our relationship with Him, and sometimes even prophetic words, God will comfort us.

When we have a personal word from God about our future or destiny, we can rest even when difficulties arise. As we have seen in Paul's life, even death couldn't keep Paul from his personal destiny. At one point earlier in Acts, he was stoned and God raised him from the dead because his personal purpose had not yet been accomplished.

It's true that if we answer God's call on our lives we may suffer a great deal of tribulation. However, if we receive His word and are walking in obedience to our call, then we have very little to worry about. It is good to begin to seek God for His plan and His purpose for our lives, and then cooperate with Him, taking steps of obedience. Like Paul, no matter what comes, we can relax and rest in God.

Personal Application

Personalize these verses and pray them for yourself and your family or friends with whom you pray. Seek His purposes and plans for your life, then ask Him to help you to be obedient and ask Him, in prayer, to bring it to pass.

Jeremiah 29: 11-13 (NIV)

For I know the plans I have for you, declares the LORD, plans to prosper you and not to harm you, plans to give you hope and a future. Then you will call upon me and come and pray to me, and I will listen to you. You will seek me and find me when you seek me with all your heart.

Matthew 11:28-30 (NKJV)

Come to Me, all you who labor and are heavy laden, and I will give you rest. Take My yoke upon you and learn from Me, for I am gentle and lowly in heart, and you will find rest for your souls. For my yoke is easy and My burden is light.

Focus Questions

1. Compare Paul's night vision in Acts 23:11 with those in Acts 16:9 and 18:9-11. What is similar? What is different?

_____

_____

_____

_____

_____

_____

2. What impact do you think the prophetic warnings of imprisonment had on Paul during more than two years in custody?

_____

_____

_____

3. Who protected Paul from the death threats of the Jews?

_____

4. How did God bring guidance and comfort to Paul during his imprisonment?

_____

_____

_____

_____

---

5. What did the word of God confirm to Paul?

_____

_____

_____

_____

6. Compare Acts 24:23 and Genesis 39:21-23. What does this say about God's sovereignty and favor during difficult circumstances?

_____

_____

_____

_____

Prayer

Dear God, show me Your plan for my life. I pray, as Paul did, for a Spirit of wisdom, revelation and understanding in the knowledge of You. Lord, help me to understand Your plans and to cooperate with them. Forgive me for times when I have been distracted or running from You, Lord. Show me what You'd like me to do, and give me the power of Your Holy Spirit to do it. Speak to me Lord, and help me to listen to Your voice. I pray that Your will would be done in my life. Help me to enter Your rest, to relax and trust You, no matter what comes in my life, in Jesus' name. Amen.

Personal Thoughts/My Response to What I Learned

_____

_____

_____

_____

_____

_____

_____

_____

_____

_____

_____

_____

_____

_____

_____

Acts 25 & 26
I WAS NOT DISOBEDIENT TO THE HEAVENLY VISION
Topic: Witnessing

Introduction: Chapter 25

In the end of Acts 23 and in Acts 24, we saw the plan of God unfolding in Paul's life despite great discomfort and tribulation for him. God protected Paul, even during his captivity by the Roman officials. God kept Paul from execution by the Jews, and used Paul as a witness to the Jews. Paul was left in the custody of the Roman officials in Jerusalem for over two years. The prophetic words that had come to Paul prepared him for his imprisonment and preaching while in custody. No doubt his disciples were praying for Paul during his imprisonment, and he was receiving strength from the Holy Spirit through their prayers. Paul knew the revealed purpose of God for his life, so he was not emotionally or spiritually defeated, even during a period of long imprisonment.

Now we see Paul, in Acts 25-26, give a defense and his personal conversion testimony before the Governor. Remember that Paul had received a direct word from the Lord two years earlier, in Acts 23:11, saying, *"Be of good cheer, Paul, for as you have testified for Me in Jerusalem, so you must also bear witness at Rome."* The power of the word from the Lord had kept Paul from despair and now his appeal to Caesar (the ruler of the Roman Empire in Rome) begins to bring it to pass. We pick up the story with the set up in Acts 25 where the Roman Governor is hearing the charges by the Jews against Paul. In this section, we survey a continuing story that encompasses both chapters 25 and 26 of the book of Acts.

FOCUS POINT
Prophetic words inspired by the Holy Spirit come true.

Read Acts 25:1-12

KEY POINTS
1. Paul appeals his case to Caesar in Rome, rather than going back to Jerusalem to face judgment.
2. Recall that Paul had received words from the Holy Spirit about this situation, as well as prophetic confirmations through other people.
3. Re-read the following verses: Acts 21:4; Acts 21:9-14; Acts 22:17-21; Acts 23:11

Introduction: Chapter 26
Paul avoids a trap that the unbelieving Jews try to set for him while trying to bring him to judgment in Jerusalem. Paul uses his legal skills to avoid going from Caesarea back to Jerusalem. (Remember that Rome occupied Palestine at this time, so Roman officials were in charge of that territory, and that the Jews of Jerusalem, with the consent of the Roman-appointed King Herod, had put Jesus to death.) Paul appeals to Caesar in Rome and avoids what would have been a sure death through an ambush on his way to Jerusalem. Again we see the hand of God providentially protecting Paul so that he can fulfill his God ordained destiny. He begins his testimony and self-defense in Acts 26. For the third time in

Acts, Paul shares an account of his previous persecution of Christians, and of his conversion to Christ on the road to Damascus.

FOCUS POINT
God uses visionary experiences to communicate with people and change the direction of their lives.

Read Acts 26:12-23

KEY POINTS
1. Look again at some of the manifestations detailed in Paul's conversion account:
   - *"I saw a light from heaven, brighter than the sun"*
   - *"when we all had fallen to the ground"*
   - *"I heard a voice speaking to me"*
2. The other accounts of Paul's conversion are found in Acts 9:1-19 and again in Acts 22:6-21.
3. Here we see Paul sharing his own testimony as he bears witness to the Lord Jesus Christ. The most powerful witnessing tool we have is the testimony of what God has done in our lives and the power of the blood of Jesus.
4. Acts 26:22
   Paul said he continues *"witnessing both to small and great..."*
5. Paul knew that what he had seen and heard in the realm of the Spirit was more lasting and important than his earthly circumstances. He boldly declared that he *"was not disobedient to the heavenly vision."*

For Deeper Study
The Christian's testimony

A Christian's testimony is a powerful tool of spiritual warfare against the adversary. Read Revelation 12:7-11. The defeat of Satan is prophesied this way: *"And they overcame him by the blood of the Lamb and by the word of their testimony..."*

Acts 1:8 tells us the purpose of the baptism of the Holy Spirit: *"for you shall receive power when the Holy Spirit has come upon you; and you shall be* witnesses *to Me in Jerusalem, and in all Judea and Samaria, and to the end of the earth."*

It is only in the power of the Holy Spirit that we can bear witness to the Lord Jesus Christ with any great effectiveness. We can, as Paul did, overcome false accusations against us by the blood of the Lamb and the word of our testimony. We can also win people to Christ with the evidence of our changed lives.

According to the *New Spirit-Filled Life Bible,* page 1539, the definition of the word *witnessing:* martureo, (mar-too-reh-oh) Strong's #3140, is as follows: "Giving evidence, attesting, confirming, confessing, bearing record, speaking well of, giving a good report, testifying, affirming that one has seen, heard, or experienced something. In the NT it is used particularly for presenting the gospel with evidence. The English word *martyr* comes from this word, suggesting that a witness is one willing to die for his testimony."

For Deeper Study

According to the *New Spirit Filled Life Bible,* page 1538, here are some visionary experiences surrounding Paul's conversion:

- Stephen's stoning 7:55,58, 59
- Paul's experience near Damascus 9:3
- Paul's vision 9:11, 12
- Ananias' visions 9:10-17

FOCUS POINT

The Holy Spirit gives supernatural grace and wisdom to believers who face accusation and persecution for their faith.

Read Acts 26:24-32

KEY POINTS

1. Paul is accused of madness by King Agrippa.
2. It is determined by the Roman officials that Paul has done nothing deserving of death or chains, but due to his appeal to Caesar, he is sent to Rome. This is a fulfillment of the prophecies spoken by the Holy Spirit to Paul.
3. While a prisoner in Rome, Paul will write his prison epistles: Ephesians, Philippians, Colossians and Philemon.
4. Paul was obedient to God. We must be obedient to God to complete our own calling and destiny.
5. Notice how <u>respectful</u> Paul is in verse 25: *"I am not mad most noble Festus."*

Personal Application

Write a short testimony of your conversion, healing, or another time when you were greatly impacted by the goodness of God.

Make a short list of particularly memorable ways that the Holy Spirit has guided you or intervened in a circumstance of your life. Ask God to help you remember those instances, then praise Him!

Focus Questions

1. Read Acts 21:4, 9-14; 22:17-21; 23:11. After two years of Paul's imprisonment, how does Festus' statement in Acts 25:12 fulfill these prophetic words?

_____

_____

_____

_____

---

2. List three manifestations Paul experienced on the road to Damascus as detailed in verses 13-14. In verse 22, what does Paul say he is doing?

    _____

    _____

    _____

3. Read Revelation 12:7-11. According to this passage, how will believers overcome Satan?

    _____

    _____

4. Read Acts 1:8. What is the purpose of the outpouring of the Holy Spirit?

    _____

    _____

5. Read Proverbs 9:10 and 29:25. What do these verses say to you about the fear of the Lord and the fear of man?

    _____

    _____

Prayer

Lord, Your Word says that I shall receive power when the Holy Spirit comes upon me, to be Your witness. I pray that You would fill me with power from on high, to be a witness for You. Father, I repent for the times that I have been timid and fearful and not done what You have impressed in my heart to do. I ask You, today, to cleanse me with the blood of Jesus and forgive my sin of fearing man. Lord, Your Word says that the fear of the Lord is the beginning of wisdom. Help me to fear You, rather than people. Please give me divine appointments, and appointed places and times during the course of my everyday life, in which I might be a witness for You. Lord, there are people all around me who are perishing, help me to reach them with the Good News of the Gospel. Lord, Your Word says that You use the weak things of this world to confound the wise and the proud, so I pray that You would use me, just as I am, for it is in Jesus' name that I pray. Amen.

Personal Thoughts/My Response to What I Learned

_____

_____

_____

_____

_____

_____

_____

_____

_____

Acts 27
AN ANGEL OF GOD STOOD BESIDE PAUL
Topics: Angelic Visitation, Prophecy

Introduction
In Acts 25 and 26, we learned about the legal proceeding in which Paul testified to the Roman governor and other officials in Caesarea. Then we saw Paul powerfully testifying to his early life and conversion to Christ through a supernatural vision and encounter with Jesus. Paul preached to his captors by the power of the Holy Spirit. He was a witness to the Lord Jesus Christ, as Jesus promised in Acts 1:8. Paul refuted the accusation of madness by the pagan ruler and witnessed powerfully for Christ. Having appealed to Caesar, in Acts 27 he is being sent out to Rome, the capital city of the Roman Empire. We begin the story of Paul's 2,000-mile journey as he boards the ship. We will see the guidance of the Holy Spirit playing a key role in Paul's fate on his journey.

FOCUS POINT
Prophecy is sometimes given by believers for the welfare of unbelievers.

Read Acts 27:1-12

KEY POINTS
1. Acts 27:10

   Paul prophesies the destruction he believes lies ahead, but his prophecy is ignored.

FOCUS POINT
God can use angels to deliver prophetic words of encouragement.

Definitions: Gifts of the Spirit

Gift of Prophecy
Characteristics of New Testament prophecy are best described in 1 Corinthians 14:3, *"But he who prophesies speaks edification and exhortation and comfort to men."* This is a God-given word for a person that is meant to "build up" (edify), "stir up" (exhort), and "cheer up" (comfort).

Read Acts 27:13-26

KEY POINTS
1. Acts 27:21

   Paul reminds those on the ship that he told them they would face disaster on this trip, as a way of pointing out that the God whom he served is living, and is one who speaks and prophesies.
2. Paul had evidently been praying for his shipmates. God responds to Paul's intercession and sends

an angel with a new word.

3. Despite the fact that they had ignored Paul, he encourages them with the angel's visitation and prophetic word.

4. Here are some key facts about the angel in Paul's visitation:

    • The angel stood beside and was seen by Paul. He had some sort of physical or visible presence.

    • The angel spoke to Paul. The angel had a voice.

    • The angel delivered the message from God, and nothing else.

5. Paul did not have a long conversation with the angel, or worship the angel in any way, but received the message with a believing heart and boldly declared the message as a prophetic word to the sailors the next day.

The Angel's Visit to Paul
Biblical Wisdom on Angelic Visitation

The *Hayford Bible Handbook* (p. 342) contains the following excellent bit of wisdom regarding angelic visitation.

"I believe God that it will be just as it was told to me (Acts 27:25)*."* Paul's certainty concerning the desperate circumstances of the ship is based on an angelic encounter with a message from God (vv. 23-24). This confidence is based on the operation of spiritual discernment (1 Cor. 12:10) as a gift from God, and the maturity of walking with God for years. *"Angels of light"* (demons, 2 Cor. 11:14) can mislead unbelievers and neophytes in the faith. Angelic messages can only be certified through

  1. consistency with the Bible,
  2. confirmation of personal witness already present in the believer,
  3. discernment given by the Holy Spirit, and
  4. confirmation of the elders in the Body of Christ.

Extrabiblical revelation, bizarre behavior outside of God's pattern of dealing with a person, and messages unsubstantiated by mature leadership who 'judge' (1 Cor. 14:29) are to be rejected.

---

6. Paul was not kept *from* the storm, but was kept safe by God in the *midst* of the storm.
    Acts 27:20 says that *"at last all hope was gone"* because the storm had raged for many days. Think about the trauma of being on that ship. Paul had been imprisoned for his faith, and now he and the others were probably sea sick, fighting for their lives in the storm. In the natural realm, they had given up hope. God did not relieve Paul's suffering, but neither did he abandon Paul in the midst of his suffering. God was with Paul and He made it clear through the angelic visitation.

For Deeper Study
Knowing the Word in Times of Trouble

Paul, who was a Pharisee and had studied the Word found in the Old Testament, doubtless knew David's words in the Psalms. Meditate on these words. Write them down, memorize them, and pray them for yourselves and others.

- Psalm 27:1-6
- Psalm 18:10-19
- Psalm 121:1-7

FOCUS POINT

We must mix prophetic words with faith.

Read Acts 27:27-44

KEY POINTS

1. Paul had heard from God, he believed what God said, and he acted on that belief.

2. Acts 27:31-34

   Paul is prophetically encouraging the sailors (his captors) and telling them what to do, as the Holy Spirit guides him. This time, they believe Paul's prophetic exhortations.

3. Look again at Acts 16:25-36.

   This is another instance of Paul encouraging his captors and turning them toward the Lord.

4. Paul did not hate his captors, but he spoke to them with respect and honor. God used him to do mighty miracles among them, to prophesy and to convert them to Christ, in some cases. He had a bigger view than his own comfort or safety. He also displayed an attitude of honor when he was a captive in Jerusalem, as was displayed in Acts 26:25 when he says things like, *"most noble Festus."*

5. God kept Paul and the others safe during the shipwreck.

   Paul's and the angel's prophetic words all come to pass. The ship is wrecked, as Paul had told them it would be, but not one life was lost. Paul had a Roman guard named Julius, with whom he had gained favor. Rather than killing Paul and the other prisoners, Julius made sure that the prisoners were protected.

Personal Application
Forgiveness

Matthew 6:14 says, *"For if you forgive men their trespasses, your heavenly Father will also forgive you."*

Ask the Holy Spirit to search your heart and show you anyone you need to forgive. Forgiveness doesn't call evil good, it just leaves the judgment to God. When you forgive others, you set yourself free.

Focus Questions

1. Looking at verse 10, what did Paul say would happen on the journey to Rome?

    _____

    _____

    _____

2. How do you think Paul was given this revelation?

    _____

    _____

    _____

3. As you read verses 21-23, what were some characteristics of the angel's message to Paul?

    _____

    _____

    _____

    _____

    _____

4. Did God keep Paul from suffering?

    _____

5. What do you think was the role of Paul's personal prayers, and those of the disciples of Paul, during this situation?

    _____

    _____

    _____

    _____

6. How did Paul react to the prophetic word from the angel?

    _____

    _____

    _____

7. How did the attitude of Paul's Roman captors change from his first declaration in Acts 27:10-11 and the situation in Acts 27:23-27?

    _____

    _____

    _____

    _____

Personal Application
The Mountains and Valleys of the Christian Walk

Read 2 Corinthians 11:16-12:10.

Great suffering and persecution often accompany great revelation. What are you going to do with the suffering of the Christian life? The Bible teaches us to display an attitude of grace and forgiveness and love toward our enemies. That is only possible through the empowerment of the Holy Spirit. When we choose forgiveness over bitterness and unforgiveness, we can walk in Christian victory. Some examples in the Bible are:

- Jesus' words in Luke 23:34.
- Stephen's words in Acts 7:60.
- Joseph's captivity as recounted in Acts 7:9-16 (summarized from Genesis 39-56).

---

8. What does this section in 2 Corinthians say to you about your own Christian walk?

_____

_____

_____

9. How does the attitude of Jesus, Stephen and Paul (as reflected in the above Personal Application passages), demonstrate Jesus' command in Luke 6:28-29 to *"bless those that curse you"*?

_____

_____

_____

Prayer
Lord, help me to trust You through the difficult circumstances of life. Help me to seek You, to hear from You, to believe You and to obey You when I walk through difficult times. Lord I pray for Your revelation. Paul heard from You and I need to hear from You regarding my own life. Help me to be sensitive to Your Holy Spirit, to read Your Word and to listen for Your voice. I pray that also for the Church worldwide. May they hear from You and trust You the way Paul did. In Jesus' name I pray. Amen.

Personal Thoughts/My Response to What I Learned

_____

_____

_____

_____

_____

_____

_____

_____

Acts 28
PAUL LAID HANDS ON HIM AND HEALED HIM
Topics: Healing, Revival

Introduction
In Acts 27, we saw Paul being taken as a prisoner aboard a ship to Rome. Paul warned the crew that they should not sail, but his warnings were not heeded and a violent storm arose that lasted many days. In the midst of the storm, Paul prayed. As a result of his prayer, an angel visited him and brought a prophetic message of encouragement that he would live to stand trial before Caesar in Rome, and that the lives of every crew member would be spared. Paul prophetically declared the angel's message before the crew, and also gave instructions as to what they should and should not do. This time they listened to him. God used a Roman soldier named Julius to protect Paul's life. Despite the shipwreck during the tempest, Paul and the crew were unharmed and made it alive to the island of Malta. This fulfilled Paul's prophetic declaration of the angel's message. We begin Acts 28 with Paul and the crew finding themselves off the coast of Italy on the island of Malta.

FOCUS POINT
God's supernatural protection can keep us safe in dangerous circumstances, but we must not test God.

Read Acts 28:1-6

KEY POINTS
1. As they reached shore after the shipwreck, Paul was unharmed after he was bitten by a poisonous viper while gathering firewood. This fulfills a promise in the Psalms, as well as Jesus' words in the Great Commission, as recorded in the Gospel of Mark.

    "For he orders his angels to protect you wherever you go. They will steady you with their hands to keep you from stumbling against the rocks on the trail. You can safely meet a lion or step on poisonous snakes, yes, even trample them beneath your feet! For the Lord says, "Because he loves me, I will rescue him; I will make him great because he trusts in my name. When he calls on me I will answer; I will be with him in trouble, and rescue him and honor him. I will satisfy him with a full life and give him my salvation" (Psalm 91:11-17 TLB).

    "And then he told them, "You are to go into all the world and preach the Good News to everyone, everywhere. Those who believe and are baptized will be saved. But those who refuse to believe will be condemned. And those who believe will use my authority to cast out demons, and they shall speak new languages. They will be able even to handle snakes with safety, and if they drink anything poisonous, it won't hurt them; and they will be able to place their hands on the sick and heal them" (Mark 16:15-17 TLB).

2. Here we find Paul, who had been preaching the Gospel of Jesus Christ in the power of the Holy Spirit, now in custody for his faith. While gathering sticks for a fire, a poisonous snake bit him and

he simply shook it off into the fire. Notice that Paul was not purposefully picking up a snake, but in the midst of his ministry, he happened upon one, which he shook off and was fine.

3. In many Bible passages the use of a serpent is a figurative way to represent the enemy, Satan. In this case, however, it was a very real serpent and the Lord literally fulfilled his Word by protecting Paul from a poisonous snake bite.

For Deeper Study
Sound Scriptural Interpretation

When interpreting Scripture we must view the whole counsel of the Bible and not take verses out of context or elevate certain passages above general scriptural principles. In Luke 4:9-12, Jesus clearly states that believers should not do dangerous things on purpose.

Some early Pentecostals (and a very few today) have taken Mark 16 so literally that they included "snake handling" in their church services. This is not a well-balanced or sound scriptural application, based upon the example of the temptations of Jesus in Luke 4.

"Then Satan took him to Jerusalem to a high roof of the Temple and said, 'If you are the Son of God, jump off! For the Scriptures say that God will send his angels to guard you and to keep you from crashing to the pavement below!' (That's the devil's misuse of Psalm 91 – the devil twisted Scripture.) *Jesus replied, 'The Scriptures also say, 'Do not put the Lord your God to a foolish test'"* (Luke 4:9-11).

Jesus is not deceived by Satan's misuse of Psalm 91 in his effort to get Jesus to purposely jump off a cliff, and expect protection from God.

A more balanced view of Luke 4, Mark 16 and Psalm 91 would be to expect the Lord's protection and pray for it and claim it, as we serve Him. However, we are not to intentionally put ourselves in harm's way (e.g., picking up poisonous snakes or jumping off a cliff while praying for God's protection). Paul encountered plenty of trouble while serving the Lord, but he did not purposely sink his own ship. When the ship sank, he called on the name of the Lord, and by faith believed the angel's words to him that his life wouldn't be lost. God kept Paul safe through great difficulty.

FOCUS POINT
The healing of the sick confirms the Gospel.

Read Acts 28:7-11

KEY POINTS
1. Exactly what Jesus had prophesied in Mark 16:17 happened in Paul's ministry on Malta. He laid hands on the sick, and they recovered. Not only was the father of the island's governor healed, but all of the sick people on the island were healed! It appears that as his personal circumstances became worse, the healing gift increased in Paul's ministry.

2. Healing revival came to Malta in the midst of Paul's shipwreck. Often, when we are in dire circumstances and desperate for God, we pray more and see our faith, and the gifts of the Spirit, increase in our lives. God's presence in our lives is often most powerful in the midst of crisis, perhaps because we draw near to God during times of difficulty.

3. The *New Spirit Filled Life Bible* (NKJV), page 1543, has additional commentary on divine healing and Paul's healing ministry on Malta in Acts 28:8-9.

> Here is a reference to divine healings in spite of the fact that Luke, a physician, accompanied Paul. This fact is so troubling to critics of modern healing that some have come forth with the theory that the healings mentioned in v. 9 were the work of Luke who used medical remedies, although Luke is not mentioned by name. The theory is based on the use of the Greek word for "healing" (v. 8) therapeuo, which they insist refers to medical therapy.
>
> In fact, however, this word occurs 34 times in the NT. In 32 instances it clearly refers to divine healing, in other cases the use is general. Both words (iaomai and therapeuo) are used in reference to the same healing in Matthew 8:7-8, indicating the terms are used interchangeably in the Bible.
>
> This observation is certainly not to oppose medical treatment or to say medicine or medical aid is wrong. It is not. However, it does clarify that this test is not grounds for the substitution of medical therapy for prayer. God heals by many means: the prayer of faith, natural recuperative powers, medical aid or medicine, and miracles.

FOCUS POINT

We are called to proclaim the Gospel in spite of our circumstances.

Read Acts 28:15-30

KEY POINTS

1. During Paul's ministry, as documented in the Book of Acts, he generally shared the Gospel of Jesus Christ with Jews first. In Acts 28:17 he again gathers the local Jews. He uses Messianic prophecies from the Old Testament to persuade them that Jesus is the Christ.

2. As Paul preaches to his Jewish audience, *"some were persuaded...and some disbelieved."* Paul then, quoting Isaiah, declares that the Gospel will go to the Gentiles.

3. Paul preached the Gospel whenever he was given the opportunity, no matter the results. We also must persevere in sharing Christ with others, even though some will not believe.

For Deeper Study
Paul's Letters from Prison

During his house arrest in Rome, Paul wrote several important letters that are included in the New Testament. They are commonly referred to as his prison epistles and include Ephesians, Colossians, and Philippians, as well as personal letters, such as the one to Philemon. According to Church tradition, Paul was released after two years, and may have continued traveling on a fourth missionary journey.

Paul's difficult circumstances are to our benefit. The Book of Philippians, in particular, is a source of great encouragement on the theme of joy regardless of circumstance.

Memorize It

Memorize Matthew 10:8 and make it your own.
Memorize Philippians 4:4-7, and regularly pray it for yourself and other believers.

Focus Questions

1. Compare Paul's experience here to Mark 16:15-17, Psalm 91:11-17 and Luke 4:9-11. What do these say to you about God's promises of protection, and also His cautions about temptation?

   _____

   _____

   _____

2. What did Paul do with the snake?

   _____

3. In Scripture, Satan and his demons are often portrayed as a serpent. While Paul faced a literal serpent and shook it off, what does this say to you about what you can do when faced with demonic activity?

   _____

   _____

   _____

   _____

4. Read Mark 16:15-17, Acts 1:8, and Matthew 10:8. How does the healing revival that broke out during Paul's ministry on Malta partially fulfill these passages?

   _____

   _____

   _____

   _____

   _____

5. Paul preached the Gospel while under house arrest. Based on Paul's example, what should your attitude be during times of difficulty?

_____

_____

_____

Prayer

Father, I pray in the name of Jesus that You would help me to be like Paul and rejoice in You, no matter what my circumstance or difficulty. He did this because of Your powerful Holy Spirit's presence in his life. I need Your presence Lord! I pray that I would get my eyes off of my circumstances and my difficulties, and onto You and Your abilities. Thank You for the sacrifice You made for me on the cross, and for the power of the Holy Spirit You sent after Your ascension. I praise You and thank You for the risen Christ who dwells in all who believe. Baptize me afresh with Your Holy Spirit, that I could be a witness to Christ's resurrection wherever I go. Amen!

Personal Thoughts/My Response to What I Learned

_____

_____

_____

_____

_____

_____

_____

_____

_____

_____

_____

_____

_____

_____

_____

_____

Conclusion
Jesus Received Power, Jesus Promised Power, Jesus Sent Power

Jesus Received Power

Jesus Christ was both fully God and fully man in the flesh. As an adult believer, He chose to publicly demonstrate His faith through water baptism by immersion. (He gave all believers an example to follow.) At that time the Holy Spirit descended upon Jesus in the form of a dove (Luke 3:21-22) and He received empowerment for His earthly ministry. After overcoming Satan's temptation in the wilderness during His 40-day fast, Jesus returned in the power of the Holy Spirit to begin His public ministry.

Jesus Promised Power

As we have seen in this study, the book of Acts began with Jesus Christ giving instructions to His followers to wait for the power He would send from heaven (Acts 1:8). He then ascended to heaven and an angel appeared to His followers and told them of His future return (Acts 1:9).

Jesus Sent Power

The promised power of the Holy Spirit then came upon the 120 men and women who had gathered in the Upper Room for a multi-day prayer meeting. The sound of a mighty, rushing wind was heard in the room and what appeared to be tongues of fire sat on the head of each person. The believers then began to speak in other tongues, declaring the goodness of God. The empowering Holy Spirit gave them the supernatural ability to be witnesses for Christ.

The historical narrative continued as the once-cowardly Peter, now baptized in the Holy Spirit, preached the Pentecostal sermon to those who had gathered outside, and three thousand more people came to faith in Christ (Acts 2:14-49).

The next six chapters focus on Peter and John, along with the other disciples, being used in the power of the Holy Spirit to heal the sick, perform miracles, cast out demons, and preach the Gospel of Jesus Christ with great power and wonderful results. The Holy Spirit guided their prayers and gave each different gifts, such as the Word of Knowledge, Discerning of Spirits, Gifts of Healings and Working of Miracles, which confirmed the word they proclaimed. In short, they did what Jesus had done in His earthly ministry, just as He had promised prior to His crucifixion in John 14:12.

After Saul's (later called Paul) conversion on the Damascus road in Acts 9, the narrative focuses on his exploits, as well as those of his disciples. After his encounter with Jesus, he was filled with the Holy Spirit and walked in His power from that day on.

Throughout the remainder of the book of Acts, we saw Paul, in the Office of an Apostle, planting churches on his three major missionary journeys. He trained and led disciples to do the works of Jesus wherever he went, and later wrote letters of encouragement to those same disciples and the churches he had planted. His disciples moved in the gifts of the Spirit and many people were converted through their efforts. In the midst of the hardships he faced on his journeys, the Holy Spirit gave Paul perseverance that was beyond human capacity in order to see God's purposes fulfilled.

The book of Acts chronicles more than just Paul's life. It tells the story of the spread of the Gospel and the history of the early Church through the lives of Paul and other heroes and martyrs of the Church, including Peter, Stephen, James and more. We saw all of these historical figures in Scripture walking in great power, seeing great evangelistic harvest and revival, as well as suffering for the sake of the Gospel. The Holy Spirit was in them and guided them as they witnessed for Jesus wherever He sent them. In Acts, we saw the Gospel go out from Jerusalem, to Antioch, to Ephesus and then to Rome, just as Jesus had prophesied in Acts 1:8.

For you shall receive power when the Holy Spirit comes upon you, to be witnesses to me in Jerusalem, Judea, Samaria and to the ends of the earth.

The same power that was in those early believers can dwell in any believer today, including you. He will guide you in the same ways He guided them, if you are willing and obedient. All you have to do is ask Him and then walk in obedience to His leading.

The keys to living a powerful, effective Christian life for the Kingdom are: 1) having an obedient heart, 2) receiving the baptism in the Holy Spirit, and 3) cultivating an intimate, personal relationship with Jesus through prayer, Bible study, and fellowship with like-minded believers. As it says in Hebrews 13:8,

Jesus Christ is the same yesterday, today and forever.

Focus Questions Answer Key

BACKGROUND OF THE BOOK OF ACTS

1. What is the source of Jesus' power in His public earthly ministry?
   Being filled with the Holy Spirit.
2. List the specific things found in Luke 4:18-19 that the anointing of the Holy Spirit would empower Jesus to do.
   Preach the gospel; heal the brokenhearted; proclaim liberty to the captives; heal the sick; set at liberty those who are oppressed.
3. List the things Jesus did after receiving the power of the Holy Spirit.
   Luke 4:15 – He teaches.
   Luke 4:30 – He walks through a mob, escaping death.
   Luke 4:31-32 – He teaches.
   Luke 4:33-36 – He casts out an unclean spirit.
   Luke 4:38-39 – He heals Peter's mother-in-law.
   Luke 4:40-41 – He heals the sick by laying on of hands and casts out demons.
   Matthew 4:23 – He goes about teaching, preaching and healing the sick.
   Acts 10:38 – He is the prototype for the Spirit-filled life.

ACTS 1

1. What did Jesus say about God's timing on His future return?
   It is not for us to know the exact time of His return.
2. Why is the power of the Holy Spirit given and how is it to be used?
   To enable us to be a witness to the lost.
3. After Jesus' ascension, what was the first way that God chose to speak to His disciples?
   Through two angels.
4. Who was at the Upper Room prayer meeting? (Hint: men only, women only or both?)
   Both men and women were in the Upper Room.
5. What is the phrase that describes the relational situation in the upper room prayer meeting?
   They were praying in agreement, or in one accord.
6. What was the first thing the Apostles did before they chose a replacement for Judas?
   They prayed for God's direction.

ACTS 2

1. List the ways (visible, audible, motivational) that the Holy Spirit's presence was manifested on the Day of Pentecost.
   The sound of a mighty, rushing wind. Divided tongues of fire appeared over their heads. Believers began to speak with other tongues about the wonderful works of God.
2. According to Peter's Pentecostal sermon (quoting Joel 2:28-32), on whom will the Spirit be poured out in these last days? What will happen when the Spirit is poured out?
   Men and women, young and old. They shall all prophesy.

3. What happened to Peter immediately BEFORE he preached his Pentecostal sermon?

   He was baptized with the Holy Spirit along with the other believers in the Upper Room.

4. What was the effect of Peter's sermon on his audience?

   The whole crowd was convicted of their sin and asked Peter what they must do to be saved. About 3,000 people came to believe in Jesus Christ as the Son of God.

5. In verse 43, what did the apostles do?

   They did many signs and wonders; they shared their possessions, and many people came to faith.

ACTS 3

1. While on their way to church, the disciples were confronted with a sick man outside the temple in the public marketplace who was in need of healing. What did they do? (Compare to Jesus' story of the Good Samaritan in Luke 10:25-37.)

   They gave him their attention and received supernatural revelation (either through a Word of Knowledge or Gift of Faith) that he would be healed, and they acted on that word.

2. What did Peter say to the man who needed healing? (Compare to Paul's statement in Acts 14:8-10.)

   He commanded the man's body to be healed. "In the name of Jesus Christ of Nazareth, rise up and walk."

3. What type of supernatural revelation do you think Peter had in order to know that he was to pray for this particular man?

   This was likely a Word of Knowledge; an awareness of the Spirit's power to heal being present.

4. What action did Peter take as a result of what the Holy Spirit helped him to perceive?

   He grabbed the man and by faith pulled him up.

5. After the man was healed by the Holy Spirit's power flowing through Peter, what did Peter do?

   He preached the gospel because the miracle opened up a preaching opportunity.

ACTS 4

1. Why were Peter and John arrested?

   They taught the people and preached in Jesus the resurrection from the dead.

2. Who arrested Peter and John?

   The priests, the captain of the temple and the Sadducees.

3. What was the result of their preaching?

   5,000 people converted to Christ.

4. What was Peter filled with before he preached?

   Peter was filled with the Holy Spirit.

5. To whom did Peter give credit for healing the lame man?

   He was healed in the name of Jesus Christ of Nazareth.

6. What hindered the religious leaders from locking up Peter and John and throwing away the key? (Hint: The healed man makes the point in verse 14 and the people make the point in verse 21.)

   Seeing the healed man standing with them and seeing the reaction of the people.

ACTS 5

1. How is the revelation of Ananias' and Sapphira's sin an example of Numbers 32:23?
    Sin never remains hidden forever; eventually it is revealed. Here it was revealed to Peter.

2. Where did Ananias and Sapphira go wrong?
    They could have chosen to keep their money, but they decided to try to "look" righteous and they deliberately lied.

3. Could they say, "the devil made me do it," or did they choose to do the wrong thing?
    They chose to deliberately lie.

4. How was the sin of Ananias and Sapphira discovered?
    The Holy Spirit revealed it to Peter.

5. What gift did the Holy Spirit likely use to communicate to Peter?
    It could have been a Word of Knowledge, Gift of Prophecy, Discerning of Spirits, or a combination.

6. According to verse 14, what was the result of the signs and wonders?
    Many men and women came to the Lord.

7. How does the ministry described in Acts 5:12-16 partially fulfill what Jesus said in His last words in Acts 1:8?
    Jesus prophesied that believers would receive power to be a witness, and here we see the results of the outpouring of the Holy Spirit.

8. What did the angel do and say and what was the apostles' response?
    They opened the jail doors, guided them out of prison, and spoke an exhortation to them. The disciples acted upon the angel's word.

9. Does God use angels as an instrument of communication and deliverance for followers of Jesus Christ?
    Yes, He does.

10. Do you think that being filled with the Holy Spirit gave the disciples persistence and perseverance? Why or why not?
    Answers vary. Yes, otherwise they could not have endured the persecution.

ACTS 6 & 7

1. In Acts 6:4, on what were the Apostolic leaders to focus their duties?
    The Word of God, prayer and the ministry of the Word.

2. What were the qualifications given in Acts 6:3 for choosing leaders over the ministry of food distribution for the widows?
    Having a good reputation, full of wisdom and the Holy Spirit.

3. What were Stephen's qualifications for ministry?
    A man full of faith and the Holy Spirit.

4. What did Moses' face "look" like in Exodus 34:29-30?
    The skin of his face shone.

5. What was the appearance of Stephen's face like in Acts 6:15?
    His face looked like the face of an angel.

6. What did Stephen see or perceive in Acts 7:55-56?

He gazed into heaven and saw the glory of God and Jesus standing at the right hand of God.

7. How do Stephen's words compare to the words of Jesus in Luke 23:34?

They were virtually the same.

8. Compare these words to Jesus' instructions in the Lord's Prayer found in Matthew 6:12-15. What does this say to you about the importance of forgiveness?

Answers will vary. Extending and receiving forgiveness is the key to the Christian faith. Christians are commanded to forgive.

ACTS 8

1. What do Acts 6:3-7 and Acts 21:8-9 tell you about Philip?

He had a good reputation, was full of wisdom and the Holy Spirit. He was an evangelist with four virgin daughters who prophesied.

2. What signs followed the preaching of the Gospel in Acts 8:6-8?

Miracles; demons were exorcised; the paralyzed and lame were healed.

3. From our text, what personal characteristics of Simon show us that he is wicked?

He practiced sorcery and claimed that he was great.

4. What did Peter discern in Simon's heart after his conversion to Christ?

He wanted to purchase the gift of God. He had bitterness and iniquity in his heart.

5. What did Peter urge Simon to do about it?

Repent and pray for forgiveness.

6. List all of the ways the Holy Spirit guided Philip in this situation.

An angel was sent and spoke to him; the Holy Spirit spoke to him; and Philip is "caught away."

7. What was the result?

The Ethiopian eunuch comes to know Jesus Christ as his Savior and Lord and is immediately water baptized.

ACTS 9

1. What are four signs that physically happened to Saul and his companions in their Damascus road encounter with Jesus?

Saul sees a bright light; he hears a voice speak; he and his companions fall to the ground; Saul trembles; he is astonished; and he submits to the voice.

2. Is God a Spirit?

Yes.

3. According to John 10:3-5, should believers be able to hear His voice?

Yes.

4. How long did Saul wait after his conversion to preach Christ?

He immediately preached.

5. Based on Acts 9:40 and Matthew 9:25, what do you conclude is the role of faith when praying for the dead to be raised?

Answers will vary. People who were grieving and weeping were kept out and a few of strong faith were allowed in. Faith appears to be the key to successful prayer in raising the dead.

ACTS 10

1. What are Cornelius' personal characteristics?

   He was devout, a man who feared God, a generous giver to the poor, and prayerful.

2. Why do you think God chose Cornelius?

   Answers may vary. He knew he was an obedient man.

3. What did Cornelius see in a vision? What did he hear?

   He saw an angel of God in a vision and heard the angel speak to him.

4. What was Peter doing when he heard a voice?

   He was praying and fasting and fell into a trance.

5. What happened during the trance?

   Peter hears a voice and sees a vision that was repeated three times.

6. What did the messengers tell Peter about why they came?

   That a holy angel spoke to Cornelius, telling them to go to a specific town, to a specific address, and to a specific man.

7. What interpretation did Peter have of the vision he received?

   That all people, not just Jews, could be saved through the Gospel of Jesus Christ, and that he should not call any man common or unclean.

8. What happened while Peter was preaching?

   The Holy Spirit fell on the whole group of Gentiles. They spoke with tongues and magnified God.

9. For what divine purpose did the Holy Spirit bring Cornelius and Peter together?

   To spread the Gospel to the Gentiles.

ACTS 11

1. Review Peter's and Cornelius' experience in Acts 10 as summarized in Acts 11. Would you say they were obedient to the supernatural revelation they received?

   Yes, they obeyed the word they received.

2. Based on John 14:15 and John 14:23-24, what does Jesus say about obedience?

   Obedience flows out of your love for the Lord.

3. What promise did Jesus make to believers in John 14:25-26?

   The Father will send the Holy Spirit and He will teach believers all things, and bring to remembrance all things Jesus has said.

4. How do you see that promise fulfilled in Acts 11:16?

   As the Holy Spirit fell, Peter suddenly remembered Jesus' words, just as He had promised.

5. List and memorize the two names that Jesus uses for the Holy Spirit in John 14:16-17. What does this say to you?

   The Helper and the Spirit of Truth.

6. What does Jeremiah 17:9-10 say about your heart and your ability to deceive yourself?

   The heart is deceitful above all things and is desperately wicked.

7. What does the above verse, in conjunction with Proverbs 11:14, indicate about having other believers speak into your life?

Answers will vary. It is good to have wisdom from other believers. Christianity is not for loners.

8. What was the result of Agabus' prophecy about a coming famine in Acts 11:28?

   The church was able to prepare and send relief to believers living in the region where the famine came.

ACTS 12

1. Who harassed the church, killed James and imprisoned Peter?

   Herod, the King.

2. What do you think Peter was feeling? Do you think he was comfortable?

   Answers vary. Knowing of James' death, he was probably anxious, although he had enough peace to sleep.

3. What happened in verse 5?

   Constant prayer was offered by the Church.

4. What do you think is the relationship between verse 5 and verse 7?

   Answers may vary. Prayers to God brought angelic intervention.

5. What does the angel say and do to Peter?

   He struck Peter's side, gave him orders, and led him out of prison.

6. Is this a physical experience for Peter or just a vision?

   It is a real, physical experience, although at first, Peter didn't understand that.

7. Although God allowed James' death at the hands of Herod, in the end, where did James end up after his death?

   He ended up in heaven with Jesus because of his faith.

ACTS 13

1. What were the disciples doing?

   Ministering to the Lord and fasting.

2. What happened as the result of what they were doing?

   The Holy Spirit spoke, choosing Paul and Barnabas for a specific task.

3. Does the Holy Spirit have a voice?

   Yes, He does.

4. What did they do in verse 3?

   They laid hands on them, in prayer, before sending them out.

5. Who sent out Saul and Barnabas?

   The Holy Spirit.

6. What happens in the rest of the chapter as a result of the fasting and prayer in the first few verses? Is that ministry productive?

   They preached, confronted a sorcerer who had previously prevented an important leader's conversion, cursed the sorcerer, converted the leader, and a whole city heard the Gospel.

7. When Paul looked at the sorcerer, what did the Holy Spirit show him about that man? (See also 1 Corinthians 12:7-11 about the Discerning of Spirits.)

   That he was a deceitful, evil man, who was seeking to keep the proconsul from coming to faith in

Christ.

8. What does Paul say to the sorcerer? Does he accept sorcery as being an alternative theology or does Paul, filled with the Holy Spirit, call evil, evil?

   Paul declares that what the sorcerer is doing is evil and curses him for it, striking him blind.

9. Based upon the above passages, do you think a Christian should view or read witchcraft-themed material?

   Absolutely not.

ACTS 14

1. Using the gift list in 1 Corinthians 12:8-10, which other gift or gifts, besides the Word of Knowledge, do you think Paul was operating in? What about the lame man?

   Answers may vary. Paul had the Gifts of Healings, Working of Miracles and Word of Knowledge. The lame man had the Gift of Faith.

2. Who gives the gifts?

   The Holy Spirit.

3. Why are the gifts given?

   "For the profit of all."

4. Comparing Acts 14:9-10 to Acts 3:4, do you notice a similarity between these experiences of Peter and Paul when they encountered a sick man?

   Answers may vary. Peter looked intently, and Paul did too. They received spiritual revelation through the Word of Knowledge that the man would be healed in both instances.

5. Focusing on verse 20, what power was there in the disciples who surrounded Paul? In what gift did they operate?

   The power of the Holy Spirit. The gift of Working of Miracles.

6. Reading what Paul says in verse 22, what does this say to you about your own life and walk with Christ?

   Answers may vary. Suffering is part of life, but we can trust Christ to bring us through it.

7. Compare verse 22 to 2 Thessalonians 1:3-8. What do these verses say to you about Christian suffering?

   Answers may vary. God will bring ultimate judgment on our persecutors.

ACTS 15

1. What do Galatians 2:20-3:3 mean to you personally, both about your salvation and about spiritual growth in Christ?

   Answers vary. The same way one is saved, by God's grace through faith, is the same way Christians can become more spiritually mature.

2. How does spiritual growth and maturity come, according to Paul?

   By faith, not by works of the flesh.

3. Can you "earn" or be "good enough" by your works, to earn salvation?

   No.

4. Should we work out disputes on our own, or should we submit ourselves to the authority of more

mature Christian leaders to help us work them out?

Submit disputes to godly counsel.

5. In what setting did the guidance of the Holy Spirit come?

The apostles and elders were together to consider the matter.

6. What was the response of the church in Antioch when the apostles (in a meeting known as the Jerusalem Council) issued their decision?

They sent out men with Paul to verbally share their written decision.

7. Read Proverbs 11:14. What does this verse say to you about seeking godly advice?

Answers vary. It is a good idea because none of us perfectly follow the Holy Spirit's guidance on our own.

8. Read Matthew 18:15-17. What are the steps to take when there is a dispute or an offense between two believers?

Step 1: Go alone. Step 2: Go with another believer. Step 3. Bring it before the whole church.

9. How did Paul and Silas resolve their conflict?

They made the decision to part ways.

ACTS 16

1. Find three ways that the Holy Spirit guided the missionaries.

1) They were forbidden by the Spirit to preach the word in Asia.

2) The Spirit did not permit them to go to Bithynia.

3) A vision appeared to Paul.

2. How is this an example of Proverbs 3:5-7?

Answers vary. Paul was trusting God to direct his path, and He did.

3. Once it became clear that they were to go to Macedonia, did Paul and Silas waste any time?

No, they immediately sought to go to Macedonia.

4. What was the first "fruit" of Paul & Silas' obedience?

The conversion of Lydia and her whole household, the deliverance of the demon-possessed girl, and the conversion of the Philippian jailer.

5. Based on the Acts 16 accounts of the possessed woman's deliverance and Lydia's conversion, do you think women are important to God?

Yes, these two stories highlight the care and concern of God for women.

6. What did Lydia do after her conversion?

She was baptized and opened her home to Paul.

7. What did the spirit of divination allow the slave girl to do?

Tell fortunes.

8. What spiritual gift did Paul display in this passage and in Acts 13:9-12? (Hint: See 1 Corinthians 12:4-11.)

The gift of Discerning of Spirits.

9. How do you think the praises of Paul and Silas affected their situation?

Answers may vary. Since Israel's complaining kept them in the wilderness for forty years, I'd suggest that Paul and Silas choosing to praise God and sing hymns after being beaten and whipped, actually released the miraculous power that set them free.

ACTS 17

1. Read Luke 18:1-8. What does this passage say to you about continuing in prayer?

   Just as we are to continue in our mission, we are to continue in prayer.

2. How did Paul show persistence in his mission?

   He didn't quit, even after being beaten and jailed. He persevered.

3. In looking at the Scriptures above, what is God's view of women in the Church?

   Women have been important since the beginning and have a role to play alongside men in the furtherance of the Gospel.

4. Compare Acts 17:4 to 17:32-34. What was the difference in the result of the ministry at Macedonia versus Athens?

   At Macedonia a great multitude believed. At Athens, some mocked, some men joined, and some wanted to hear more.

ACTS 18

1. What was Paul's occupation?

   He was a tentmaker (and possibly a leatherworker).

2. Who did God send to work alongside Paul?

   Aquila and Priscilla.

3. What was Paul "compelled" to do by the Holy Spirit?

   He testified to the Jews that Jesus is the Christ.

4. Looking back in Acts 1:8, what is the purpose for which the Holy Spirit is given?

   To be a witness for Jesus.

5. In Acts 18:9, how did the Lord speak to Paul?

   He spoke to Paul in the night by a vision and a voice.

6. Personal Reflection: Consider a time when you received clear guidance from the Lord. Write a brief testimony of that experience.

   Answers vary. Find a time to share your personal testimony with someone .

ACTS 19

1. Whom did Paul encounter as he came through Ephesus?

   Some local disciples.

2. What question did Paul ask them?

   Did you receive the Holy Spirit when you believed?

3. What happened after these disciples were re-baptized in water, and then the apostle laid his hands upon them?

   They spoke with tongues and prophesied.

4. What experience is common in Acts 2:4, Acts 10:44-48 and Acts 19:5-6?

   Speaking in tongues.

5. What two things happened through Paul's hands, and even through articles of his clothing in Acts 19:11-12?

Unusual miracles were done so that diseases were healed and evil spirits left people upon whom Paul laid his hands.

6. In Mark 16:14-18, what five signs did Jesus say would follow those who believe?
They would cast out demons, speak with new tongues, take up serpents, drink any deadly thing and it won't hurt them, lay hands on the sick and they will recover.

7. What happened to the unbelievers who tried to use the name of Jesus to exorcise a demon when they didn't know Jesus by faith?
The demon beat them up.

8. Personal Reflection: Consider Acts 19:5-6, 19:11-12, and Mark 16:17-18 and what this says to you as a believer. Are you experiencing this yet in your walk with Jesus? If not, how do you think you can begin to experience these things?
Answers vary. Get prayed for by a trustworthy apostolic leader, pray in tongues more frequently, pray and ask for a fresh outpouring of the Holy Spirit.

9. How could the scene in Ephesus be described as being motivated by spiritual warfare (the invisible battle between Satan's demonic spirits and God's holy angels) played out in an earthly scene?
Answers vary. The mob was stirred up by idol-makers who (knowingly or unknowingly) were followers of Satan. By the power of the Holy Spirit, Paul preached against idols in favor of worshipping one true God. He became the target of the idol-makers' wrath as people were turned away from idol worship. No doubt the demonic spirits of the idolaters were causing the crowd to riot and great confusion was evident. Holy angels would have been battling to protect Paul in the unseen realm.

ACTS 20 & 21

1. What spiritual gifts do you think were in operation when Paul raised a man from the dead?
Gift of Faith, Gift of Working of Miracles.

2. What Ephesians 4:11 ministry office did Philip hold? What does the text say about his daughters?
Office of the Evangelist. His daughters all prophesy.

3. What did all the prophetic words warn Paul about if he went to Jerusalem?
That he will be bound in chains in Jerusalem.

4. What was Paul's response?
He goes to Jerusalem anyway.

5. Personal Reflection: Have you ever received confirmation through an accurate prophetic word from another person? Share a brief personal testimony.
Answers vary.

ACTS 22

1. In what ways did Jesus manifest His presence in Paul's conversion?
With a bright light, Paul trembling and falling to the ground, and through a voice.

2. Was there a time when you were overwhelmed with the Lord's presence in a very tangible, physical way? Briefly explain the situation in a short, personal testimony if you have one.
Answers vary. Share experiences as time permits if studying in a group format.

3. Compare Acts 10:10-13 and Acts 11:5 with Acts 22:17-21 What happened to both Peter and Paul while they fell into a trance during prayer?

   Paul had a conversation with a voice that told him to leave Jerusalem and go to the Gentiles. Peter saw a vision and heard a voice and had a conversation. Both were sent to the Gentiles.

4. How did God sovereignly protect Paul from the angry mob?

   Paul was actually rescued by being arrested by the Romans and brought into their barracks.

5. Looking back at Acts 21:10-11, did that prophecy by Agabus come true?

   Yes, Agabus' word of exhortation to Paul about impending imprisonment came true, along with other warnings Paul had received.

6. How did God use Paul's natural knowledge to keep him safe when in the Roman barracks?

   Paul was kept safe when he asserted his Roman citizenship in order to avoid being beaten. Paul knew the Roman legal system and used it to his advantage.

ACTS 23 & 24

1. Compare Paul's night vision in Acts 23:11 with those in Acts 16:9 and 18:9-11. What is similar? What is different?

   In 16:9 the text indicates he saw a man in a vision. In 18:9 the Lord spoke in the night by a vision. Here it states the Lord stood by Paul in a vision. The first gave Paul direction, the second two brought reassurance.

2. What impact do you think the prophetic warnings of imprisonment had on Paul during more than two years in custody?

   He would remember that God had warned and prepared him for difficulty and take comfort from that.

3. Who protected Paul from the death threats of the Jews?

   Paul's sister's son, his nephew.

4. How did God bring guidance and comfort to Paul during his imprisonment?

   The Lord stood by Paul in the night and spoke comforting words to him.

5. What did the word of God confirm to Paul?

   That he would live long enough to testify in Rome.

6. Compare Acts 24:23 and Genesis 39:21-23. What does this say about God's sovereignty and favor during difficult circumstances?

   Both Joseph and Paul were imprisoned despite doing no wrong, and were said to walk in favor.

ACTS 25 & 26

1. Read Acts 21:4, 9-14; 22:17-21; 23:11. After two years of Paul's imprisonment, how does Festus' statement in Acts 25:12 fulfill these prophetic words?

   It was prophesied that Paul would be imprisoned, but that he would be a witness to the Gentiles.

2. List three manifestations Paul experienced on the road to Damascus as detailed in verses 13-14. In verse 22, what does Paul say he is doing?

   He saw a bright light, he fell to the ground, and heard a voice speaking to him. He is witnessing to everyone.

3. Read Revelation 12:7-11. According to this passage, how will believers overcome Satan?
   By the blood of the Lamb and the word of our testimony.

4. Read Acts 1:8. What is the purpose of the outpouring of the Holy Spirit?
   Believers would receive power to be a witness for Jesus Christ.

5. Read Proverbs 9:10 and 29:25. What do these verses say to you about the fear of the Lord and the fear of man?
   In the fear of the Lord is wisdom and safety, but the fear of man brings a trap or snare.

ACTS 27

1. Looking at verse 10, what did Paul say would happen on the journey to Rome?
   He said that disaster would come, along with loss of cargo and life. Note that Paul was only partially right.

2. How do you think Paul was given this revelation?
   Answers may vary. Through prophetic insight.

3. As you read verses 21-23, what were some characteristics of the angel's message to Paul?
   The angel stood next to Paul and spoke with an audible voice. The word the angel spoke was concise and was clearly prophetic encouragement and exhortation. Note that it was not a lengthy conversation, nor did the angel accept worship. In short, the angel reassured Paul that he wasn't going to die in a shipwreck.

4. Did God keep Paul from suffering?
   No.

5. What do you think was the role of Paul's personal prayers, and those of the disciples of Paul, during this situation?
   Answers may vary. Paul most likely saw the potential for loss of life in this situation and prayed earnestly for himself and his shipmates. Doubtless the prayers had made a difference and spared the lives of the sailors and brought about the angel's visit.

6. How did Paul react to the prophetic word from the angel?
   He believed it and declared it by faith.

7. How did the attitude of Paul's Roman captors change from his first declaration in Acts 27:10-11 and the situation in Acts 27:23-27?
   At first, Paul's words were ignored. However, after the storm had begun and worsened, and Paul's words came true, their attitude toward Paul changed. They listened to Paul.

8. What does the passage in 2 Corinthians 11:16-12:10 say to you about your own Christian walk?
   Answers may vary. Suffering for Christ's sake is part of the Gospel.

9. How does the attitude of Jesus, Stephen and Paul (as reflected in the above Personal Application passages), demonstrate Jesus' command in Luke 6:28-29 to *"bless those that curse you"*?
   They were all able to look past the persecution brought by their enemies, and forgive and bless them.

ACTS 28

1. Compare Paul's experience here to Mark 16:15-17, Psalm 91:11-17 and Luke 4:9-11. What do

these say to you about God's promises of protection, and also His cautions about temptation?
Answers will vary. God promises His people protection when they are serving Him. However, we must not purposefully do dangerous things, thereby testing God.

2. What did Paul do with the snake?
He shook it off into the fire.

3. In Scripture, Satan and his demons are often portrayed as a serpent. While Paul faced a literal serpent and shook it off, what does this say to you about what you can do when faced with demonic activity?
Answers may vary. Do not focus on the enemy's attack, simply shake it off.

4. Read Mark 16:15-17, Acts 1:8, and Matthew 10:8. How does the healing revival that broke out during Paul's ministry on Malta partially fulfill these passages?
The prophesied power of the Holy Spirit was with Paul as he traveled and preached. In the name of Jesus he healed the sick and raised dead people. These signs were evidence that the kingdom of God was at hand.

5. Paul preached the Gospel while under house arrest. Based on Paul's example, what should your attitude be during times of difficulty?
Answers vary. We are to preach Christ no matter what the circumstances are.

TESTIMONIES
God Speaks Today

Table of Contents

God Speaks Through a Child
April Amiot

I believe that children are able to hear more clearly from God than adults do. We had been trying to have a second child for around three years, but with no success. Taylor, our four-year-old son, knew that we were praying for a baby. He had his heart set on having a baby sister, and he wanted her to be named "Emmie." In fact, he wanted a baby sister so badly that he played with an imaginary sister named Emmie, though sometimes Emmie was also an imaginary cat. He was so certain that he would have a sister named Emmie that I would have to forewarn all his new Sunday School teachers that I was not pregnant, no matter how much Taylor insisted that his baby sister was going to use his old crib or car seat.

One day my sister Aimee and I were taking Taylor to the zoo. Suddenly, from the back seat of the car we heard Taylor's little voice pipe up with excitement, "Oh NOW I know what Jesus wants!"

Aimee and I looked at each other and I asked Taylor, "What does Jesus want?"

"Jesus wants us to pray for my baby sister NOW!" he exclaimed.

Fully believing him, we pulled the car over to the side of the road and right there outside the zoo we prayed for Taylor's baby sister Emmie to come. When we were done praying he announced confidently, "She'll be here by my birthday."

By the time his next birthday rolled around I was about to pop, being nearly nine months pregnant with our little girl. Of course, we named her Emma.

We remind our children that we prayed for them and that God heard our prayers. We remind them of this story when they are fighting (haha)! And we remind them when we are trying to make them feel special and loved. God knew the desires of our hearts. In fact, God GAVE us those desires in the first place, and then He delighted to fulfill them using the prayers and faith of a four-year-old boy.

April Amiot is a happy wife and mother of three children. Trained as an English teacher, she and her family are currently missionaries and live in San Jose, Costa Rica. She can be reached at www.amiotfamily.org.

A Crazy Leap of Faith
Connie Bendickson

In October 2008, our family took a crazy leap of faith. We sold our house, bought a motorhome, and drove away from the life we'd always known. The thought of leaving our home and living in an RV wasn't on our radar even one year before we hit the road. We'd never been campers except one weekend a year when we'd join our college friends for an annual trip. We were perfectly happy with life and we weren't looking to make any major changes. Leaving our life behind to hit the camping scene was certainly not something we ever expected to do.

Our typical family vacations usually involved non-stop air travel and rental cars. But in August 2007, we took our first long-distance road trip driving our minivan from Minneapolis to Seattle. We discovered that we *loved* the open road and the slower pace. We had a blast together! I can see now that God was giving us a taste of things to come.

During that summer of 2007, I began to really ponder what it meant to educate our children. What was the purpose of education? What were we trying to accomplish in 18 years? This topic consumed me that whole school year. I read, I prayed, I wondered.

All that contemplation led me to this conclusion: *What I deeply desire for our children is for them to become who God created them to be and be equipped to do what He is calling them to do.* Being who God created us to be is how we glorify God. My job as a mother is to help my children discover who they are and to help them pursue what will prepare them for the call on their lives.

After much more prayer – and with some fear and trembling – we chose not to re-enroll our children in the homeshool academy they had attended since kindergarten. (They were now about to enter 6th and 3rd grade.) This was a big step for us and one of the hardest things we have ever done as we loved being part of this community. Nevertheless, we knew we had to do it, though we didn't yet know why.

God also began to untie other anchors that had held us in place. We were feeling increasingly detached from our church which, was very unusual for us. I couldn't commit to anything friends were asking us to do in the fall, such as buy concert tickets, join a homeschool group, or plan get-togethers. Deep inside I knew we wouldn't be around to do it.

I kept hearing the Lord say, "Get your house in order," and I began to clear the nooks and crannies of our home. I was preparing…that's all I knew.

Additionally, we had felt for a while that someday we would be moving from suburbia to a place with more land. We had even looked at some properties, but the timing never felt right.

These were all pieces of a puzzle that would only later fit together. We had not yet seen the big picture. We were just listening and responding to what we knew at the time, one step at a time.

As I look back, I realize that God had been preparing us for this radical move for at least a year. It had been a season of waiting on God in the unknown places. Waiting isn't always easy, but the truth is, *"Those who wait on the Lord will find new strength. They will fly high on wings like eagles. They will run and not grow weary. They will walk and not faint"* (Isaiah 40:31).

The Dream

Do you ever have dreams? Dreams that don't fade away when the light of day starts streaming into your bedroom? Dreams that wake you up in the night and beg to be understood?

I don't. At least not very often. But in April 2008 I had an incredible dream. It was so vivid and so real that it woke me up in the middle of the night.

In the dream, our family of four was floating down a calm river. All of a sudden it became a rushing river and we were scared, separated from each other, and getting tossed about. We went around a sharp turn and the river turned calm again. I remember thinking how much better it would have been if we had been together in a raft or boat. It wouldn't have been as scary and perhaps we could have enjoyed the rushing river rapids.

When I woke up I asked God to show me what the dream meant. He began to reveal to me our future.

"There is a season quickly approaching that will be like the rushing river rapids," I heard Him say. "You need to stick together as a family. The four of you need to be in the same boat traveling together. This will be a time that binds you together as a family and strengthens your trust and dependence on Me. At first it may look tempting to go directly to the land by simply cutting across the peninsula inside the hairpin curve. However, if you choose to take the short cut, you will miss out on learning how to flow with the river and you will not be prepared for what is coming next, the season after the rapids. Though it seems simple to cross the land and avoid the rapids, looks can be deceiving. There are high treacherous banks to climb and a dense forest to cross, though you cannot see that from where you are now. It would require much self-reliance and striving. It would divide your family and would not teach you the lessons you will learn from the river."

I had a strong impression that we were not to go directly to the land. Then I had a vision of our house sitting in the river like a great big cruise ship. It could not move forward. It was far too large and cumbersome to be able to flow in the river, and it looked ridiculous. We had to jump out of the ship (our house) and into a smaller boat (which we later knew was the RV) and let the river bring us to the land.

This encounter was like no other. It filled my thoughts and was in the back of my mind for months. I believe it was an invitation from God to step into an opportunity to flow with His River (the Holy Spirit). Would we accept this invitation? First, we had to count the cost. And the cost was high. So we prayed and pondered and wondered – what if we decided to let the River flow?

At the end of July, my husband Rich and I spent a week on the North Shore of Lake Superior celebrating our 20th anniversary. The summer was starting to fade and we were growing weary of living in the unknown. Throughout the week we cried out to God to make His plans clear to us for this coming year. Was it the RV or something else? Are we supposed to do this or not? We laid it all on the altar and asked God to bring clarity.

We decided to read the Scriptures from the Torah schedule for the week. As I read from Numbers 33, I was astounded at what I saw! It's a record of the Israelite's journey out of Egypt, through the desert, and into the Promised Land. Their whole itinerary is listed and it reads like this:

> *After leaving Rameses, the Israelites set up camp at Succoth.*
> *Then they left Succoth and camped at Etham...*
> *They left Etham and camped near Migdol...*

It goes on like this for 44 verses! It's their whole itinerary as they *camped* in the desert before going into the Promised Land! Verse after verse, the word "*camped*" jumped off the page at me. Could this be a picture of how God is working in our life right now? Bringing us out of Egypt (a place of slavery), through the desert (a place of testing, growing, and maturing), and then to the Promised Land where we will live to glorify Him? We believe these Scriptures were yet another way God was saying, "yes" we need to do this.

The next few weeks were filled with a sense of wonder and anticipation. Have you ever stood at the edge of a diving board with that feeling of wanting to jump off, yet not quite sure? At some level, we knew we would take this leap of faith, but there was still a feeling of, "Is this really you, God?" We had been looking at RVs off and on throughout the summer, but never very seriously. And frankly, all the choices were overwhelming. Yet, we had peace that if God was calling us to this, He would lead us to the RV for us. One Sunday night in mid-August we were looking at motor homes online. We'd looked before and debated what type would be best, but nothing ever really caught our attention. Then I saw it.

It was a 2007 Newmar All-Star and I was drawn to it like no other. Rich had already gone to bed, so I sent him an email that said, "This is it!" along with a link to the listing. I looked at the pictures, then back at the listing, and saw something I hadn't seen before. It said "sale pending."

Oh, no. What's up with that? I thought. I emailed the dealership asking if it was still available. In the morning I got a reply saying that someone had already put money down and was set to close on August 22, but if I wanted to be notified if something happened, I should let them know. I immediately said, "Yes, let me know."

Then I prayed a flippant (and apparently powerful) little prayer as I walked out of our office. "God, if that is the motor home we are supposed to have, then I pray that sale falls through."

Two hours later I got the following email:

> *Dear Connie,*
> *Guess What? The gentleman that had put the deposit on this All Star just called and cancelled his purchase. He is in the military and was notified yesterday that he was being transferred to Hawaii in six weeks.*
> *So, what can I tell you about this coach? It has TV's everywhere, In-Motion Satellite, Power Awning, Convection/Microwave Oven, low mileage, etc.*
> *I sold this coach brand new so I do know the history and what kind of work has been done to it. I even have the service records for it.*

Let me know what you think,
Susan

Wow! So *now* what do we do? We had to go see it. Rich and I flew to North Carolina that Friday, saw it on Saturday, and flew back home to Minnesota. We knew this was the one so we put an offer in on Tuesday. A couple weeks later, all four of us drove out to pick it up and bring our new home back to Minnesota.

We spent the next few weeks packing up our house and putting it on the market. We gathered our friends and family for a bon voyage party, said goodbye to life as we knew it, climbed into our new home on wheels, and drove away.

A Look Back

It was a step-by-step walk of faith that eventually led us to a place where we jumped off the diving board into the deep water. We entered the flow of God's River and allowed Him to teach us and prepare us before bringing us to the land.

To many people, this leap of faith looked a bit crazy. To tell you the truth, it felt a bit crazy to us, too. This wasn't something we set our sights on and then tried to make happen. Our nearest and dearest friends can attest to the fact that we did not head into this on a whim. It was only our sincere desire to listen to and obey God that led us here.

But the Bible tells us that God often leads His people in ways that are out of the ordinary. Whether by dreams, or visions, or a burning bush, God has unique ways of showing us the next step.

It's been nearly four years now since we traded our life on wheels for a regular home. I can tell you with great enthusiasm that we have no regrets about taking that leap of faith to walk in obedience to what God was asking us to do, even if it did seem crazy at the time. There are so many blessings that happened in the course of our two years on the road and they continue to flow as a result of that season. We learned so much about ourselves and each other. We were united as a family. We learned we can live with a lot less than we ever thought possible. We learned to trust God to lead us. And we learned so much more.

Plus, God did bring us to the land! We now live on a five acre hobby farm where the Lord has blessed us with chickens, goats, horses, two barn cats, a garden, an orchard and the potential for so much more. Dreams really do come true.

Crazy? Perhaps, but we wouldn't have it any other way.

Connie Bendickson is a wife, homeschooling mom, health food nut, lover of family and friends, and follower of Jesus. She lives with her family in Corcoran, Minnesota. You can follow Connie's blog at www.squarerootwellness.wordpress.com.

Introducing The Love of Jesus to the Woman on the Plane
Rev. Rick Black

I was flying home to Colorado from RAIN Ministries Bible Camp in Montana after ministering to many people with Pastor Damien Wong of Life Church in Kona, Hawaii. We experienced a very busy and successful time of ministry at the camp, and had seen many people emotionally, physically and spiritually healed and set free. The plane was completely full, but I got to my seat, fully intending to relax or sleep, but God had another plan.

Just as I was about to put my earphones in to listen to some music, the woman next to me began a small-talk conversation, offering me a mint. The subject turned to the camp that I'd just come from and I explained that I was a Christian minister and had just been praying for many people. She mentioned that she was a new age healer, describing some sort of therapy she was involved with to bring emotional healing to people. I asked her what her success rate was, and she admitted that it wasn't very good, sounding disappointed.

I began sharing testimonies of healings and deliverances of people we had ministered to at Bible camp. I told her that she just deals with the mind-body realm, but I deal with spirit, soul, and body. "The realm of the spirit has two kingdoms, God's kingdom and the kingdom of darkness," I told her. "And the enemy (Satan) sets people up for abuse, hurt, and disappointments. It's only Jesus Christ who can set them free from the effects of all kinds of abuse."

She was intrigued and wanted to hear more, and at that point, one particular testimony came to mind. At the Bible camp, God had physically healed a woman who had been a victim of molestation in her past. I had led her through the process of forgiving and releasing the emotional trauma in the name of Jesus Christ. We often see people set free from physical pain when we introduce Jesus Christ to them and lead them through a series of forgiveness and release exercises.

As we were talking, the woman on the airplane became emotional and started to weep. She then began to share her own personal pain and struggles with me. From what she told me, I could see a pattern of despair and disappointments in her life. She had been repeatedly abused and victimized her whole life. I then sensed she might be ready to release her pain and to receive the Lord.

Suddenly, the pilot announced we were beginning our descent into Denver, and I knew time was short. I asked her if she was ready to release the emotional pain of her past and also get rid of neck pain, back pain, and knee pain, which she had mentioned. Through her tears, she nodded that she was ready. I often use the word-picture of taking off an old, filthy garment as I explain how Jesus sends the Holy Spirit to set people free of the guilt, shame, and condemnation of their past, and that He can bring them a whole new identity.

Right there on the airplane I led her through a prayer exercise in which she visualized taking off her false identity as a wounded victim, and inviting Jesus to bring her something else to "put on." I invited her to pray, "Jesus bring me something to put on to replace what I just took off."

After she tearfully went through the exercise of taking off her old identity and getting rid of all the guilt, shame, bitterness, and unforgiveness, I asked her if Jesus was still there where she could see

Him. She nodded yes and I asked her to move face to face with Him and to take one big step right into Him. She suddenly exclaimed, "I knew it was You!"

It was as though she was talking directly to Jesus. I leaned over and said to her, "Why don't you just give your life to Jesus now."

She agreed, and I led her in a prayer to ask Jesus Christ to be her Lord and Savior. She accepted His forgiveness and His love. She told me she felt as though Jesus spoke directly to her and said, "I've been waiting all of these years for you!"

God clearly wanted to complete her healing, so I prayed for her knees, her neck, and her back, and she was completely healed of all pain. By that point, the plane had landed and she looked at me and exclaimed, "Who are you, man?" I just smiled and it was time to walk off the plane.

Pastor Rick is an ordained minister through Life Church in Kona, Hawaii, and lives in Colorado with his wife of 35 years. They have three children and ten grandchildren. Pastor Rick travels and ministers with Pastor Damien Wong when he visits the mainland. His basis for ministry is Acts 10:38 ..."who went about doing good, and healing all that were oppressed of the devil; for God was with Him." For more information about Pastor Rick and Pastor Damien's ministry, visit the church website at www.konalifechurch.org.

Jesus' Healing Love was the KEY to Their Hearts!
Rev. Bob Brasset

We recently received a request for my friend John and I to pray for healing for an East Indian Hindu family in our hometown of Victoria. When we arrived at their home we found a warm, friendly, receptive family with five school-aged children.

Their house, however, was filled with idols and pictures of living and dead Gurus. We ignored the idols and just loved the family. The fact that those idols were there didn't stop the love and compassion of Jesus from being expressed.

The father was the first to receive ministry. He said afterward, "I felt a jolt of electricity in my body when you were walking toward me and the pain left immediately."

A doctor later confirmed that he was completely healed of a hernia and a stomach/digestive problem.

The mother was next. "I have painful warts on my feet and I can't seem to get them healed," she said.

When she took off her shoes we saw that she had duct tape covering the warts on both feet. Her healing wasn't immediate, but within 10 days all the warts were gone and haven't returned.

Finally, it was their six-year-old daughter's turn. Her body was covered with eczema. The doctor had tried several remedies, but to no avail. John and I commanded the eczema to go and for normal, healthy skin to return. The result? Her skin is now normal, healthy and completely eczema-free.

After seeing these healings, the father declared spontaneously, "Jesus died on the cross. He is God. I want all of my family to know Jesus."

Soon thereafter, the father was interested in knowing Jesus more fully and learning how to pray to Him. One day he told us what happened when he lost the keys to his office.

"I was driving along in one of my taxis, desperate to get to my office because I couldn't find my office keys anywhere. I really needed those keys. As I drove along I prayed, 'Jesus, you healed me. I now believe you are God. Lord, you've got to help me find those keys!'

"I felt an immediate urge to roll down the passenger window. Then someone cut me off and I swerved and jammed on the brakes to avoid a collision. When I did, I heard a loud *crack*, like an object hitting my dashboard. I looked and there were the keys!

"I was dumbfounded. What an immediate answer to prayer! I had searched the car and knew the keys weren't there when I got in. Could I have left them on the roof of the car and God arranged to have them fly through the open window? Only He knows. I just know that He is God and He loves me!"

Bob Brasset is a passionate God-chaser. He has over 30 years of experience as a pastor/minister, conference speaker and revivalist. A member of Partners in Harvest Churches, he currently oversees Extreme Healing Ministries, an international coalition of ministries that brings healing, evangelistic and equipping teams to the nations. He lives with his wife, Sue, in Victoria, British Columbia, Canada. Learn more at www.bobbrasset.ca.

The Healing Waters of Baptism
Ron Conroy

In 2008, just as our Wednesday night service was ending, the Holy Spirit gave me a Word of Knowledge that a man (Shawn) who was to be baptized in our home pool the following Sunday afternoon, would be healed of MS (Multiple Sclerosis) in the waters of baptism.

I immediately went to the senior pastor's wife and Shawn's sponsor, and shared with them the Word of Knowledge that was given to me. The three of us joined together to pray over it and made a commitment not to tell anyone.

That Sunday, Shawn came to our home and was baptized in our pool by our senior pastor. When he came out of the pool, he said nothing about anything he had experienced during his baptism.

One month later, Shawn went to his doctor for a regular check-up and was tested to see how his MS had progressed. To their amazement, the doctors could find no trace of MS remaining in his system.

Six months later, Shawn returned to the doctor, and when he went through the testing again, there was still no trace of MS in his system.

Shortly after this doctor appointment, Shawn came to my office to work on my computer systems (he is a computer systems technician). It was during that visit that Shawn told me of his good news – there was no MS in his body! I asked how this could have happened, and he told me his story.

"When I came up out of the waters of baptism," he said, "I felt a warmth come over my body that I had never felt before. It was a soothing warmth, and immediately I felt better, and continued to feel better. So much so, that I went to the doctor to be tested for what was happening in my body. It was there the doctor discovered there was no trace of MS in my system. Six months later there is still no trace of MS in my system. The doctors can't explain it, but I know I was healed in the waters of baptism."

It was then I shared with Shawn that the Holy Spirit had given me a Word of Knowledge that God was going to heal him of MS when he was baptized.

Today, Shawn is happily working, still free of MS.

Ron Conroy asked Jesus Christ into to be the Lord and Savior of his life in 1972. Since then, he has been a witness to the Good News of Jesus Christ within the church walls as well as in the business community. Ron has the boldness to take conversational phrases and turn them into witnessing opportunities. He follows the leading of the Holy Spirit, prays for people to open the door to their heart, and then speaks the Word of Life into them. He has taken the Word to his businesses, employers, fellow employees, and anyone that crosses his path. He is an active witness for Christ and understands that the grace of God has covered all his failings. He can be reached at ron@conroyconsult.com.

The Promised Healing
Nancy Dobbs

As I was preparing to go on a mission trip to help children in Columbia, I received a special Word of Knowledge about the eyes of a young girl being healed. Not knowing how that would be fulfilled, or if it even referred to my trip, I continued my packing and left for the mission field.

The children we found there, many of whom were orphans, lived in very needy situations. We were part of a team called *Love in Action! Faith that Works!* Our group was able to touch hundreds of children with the love of Jesus which was demonstrated in many practical ways. We distributed supplies, toys and clothing; gave away hugs and kisses; and shared Bible verses, encouragement and prayers.

In return, we received such a blessing! We were touched by the joyous laughter of the children, their little hands reaching out to receive a touch, an embrace, or a butterfly sticker. Their faces—some dirty, some with shining eyes—were full of excitement and full of need. I was reminded how blessed my own children are in America.

But two young girls stood out from all the rest. I can still picture the sweet faces of these two sisters standing before me with their little eyes blinking uncontrollably. From birth they had struggled with this incurable condition. As I looked at them my heart was touched in a way that Jesus must have been touched when He encountered someone in need.

I remembered the Word of Knowledge I received before the trip regarding the healing of a young girl's eyes. And now, days later, not one but two little hearts full of faith were in front of me. I wondered, *Could this be the promised healing?* With expectant, sweet faith, the oldest asked, "Would you pray and ask Jesus to heal our eyes?"

We prayed with faith, and He faithfully answered. Two little girls rejoiced as Jesus touched their eyes with His healing presence!

Returning to this church ten days later, the older sister presented a special drawing to me with this inscription: *To the lady who prayed for me when Jesus healed my eyes.* It was special to experience this fulfillment of a Word of Knowledge, and by receiving the promise even before the trip, it produced expectant faith as we prayed for this miracle healing. The next year we met the little girls again…still rejoicing that their eyes had been healed by Jesus!

Nancy Dobbs trained in healing ministry through the International Association of Healing Rooms and Global Awakening's School of Healing & Impartation. She has college degrees and extensive training in education, design and theology. She and her husband are connected with Glory of Zion International.

The Power of His Word
Mary Harding

Early one morning a number of years ago, I was lying on my bed with my nine-month-old daughter as my husband left with our other two children. They were going to the bank for a quick errand.

As they drove away a Scripture came to mind; *"No weapon formed against you will prosper"* (Isaiah 54:17). I thought that was a good Scripture, and then the Holy Spirit brought another one to mind from Psalm 91; *"The angels of the Lord encamp around us."* Again, I thought this was another good promise of God's protection. But I had only agreed with the Word, I hadn't spoken it or prayed it.

Immediately, the Holy Spirit spoke these words to my mind, which I had never heard before. "There is creative power in the spoken Word."

Those words seemed like they were on a banner in my mind. It was a mandate. He was clearly telling me to speak those Bible verses over my husband and children while they were gone. It was like the Holy Spirit was telling me those words would not be carried out unless I spoke them out loud. It was more than a good thought. It was clear direction from God for my family that day, and I immediately spoke those Scriptures over my family who had just driven away.

It was now two hours since they had left and I had not heard from my husband. (This was before cell phones were in common use.) He was only going to drive five minutes away to the bank and then come home. It was the only thing on his list to do. Finally, the phone rang and my husband was calling me from the bank. He told me the bank had been robbed!

The man who robbed the bank had been standing in line right next to my husband. While they were waiting for their turn at the teller, my two children had been running back and forth between a kid's play area and my husband. They ran past the man who robbed the bank many times. When my husband reached the counter, he noticed the teller next to his was crying. The man had just quietly robbed the bank by handing a note with his demands to the teller. She had given him what he asked for so no one was hurt.

After the robber left, the bank was closed, locked and surrounded by policemen with guns drawn. Everyone in the bank was put on the floor for protection. After the police determined it was safe outside, everyone was finally released.

The Holy Spirit had shown me through a Word of Wisdom that the words of protection in this situation had to be spoken. He has continued to teach me what this means. The spoken word of God is our sword of the Spirit, just as in Ephesians 6:17 where the Greek language used for *word* is "rhema," which means the spoken word, and not "logos," which means the written word. Jesus gave us His authority, but we must speak it out, just like He did when He was tempted in the wilderness.

Spoken words are what God used to create the world, and what Jesus used to defeat the devil in Luke 4. Now, when the Holy Spirit brings Scriptures to mind concerning a situation, I know to speak them out and believe that God will perform them. The spoken word of God has creative power, and they are sure promises on which we can stand.

Mary Harding accepted Jesus as her Savior in early childhood and grew up with the awareness of God's presence and His faithfulness to hear her prayers. Throughout the different seasons of life, her focus has been to maintain daily fellowship with Father God through the blood of Jesus and the power of the Holy Spirit. Her goal is to grow in the knowledge of the Word of grace and to release God's life-giving power through praise in everyday situations. She desires to consistently pray for herself and others to see God's victory in every area of life through His love, His provision, and His power.

Step Out of the Boat
Pastor Dave Kaufman

In 1980, my wife and I had served only one year in full-time ministry when the Lord began to speak to us about pioneering a church. I had a Bible college degree from a Pentecostal denomination, but it seemed that God wanted us to go in a different direction.

We were Kingdom-minded people and we felt that God wanted us to start a non-denominational church. This was very rare in 1980, but we were constantly encouraged through God's Word, Christian songs, prophetic words, and Godly fellowship.

Just as the Lord gave Peter just one word ("come") when he stepped out of the boat, God was reassuring our hearts that He would sustain us. The Lord reminded us in Isaiah 55:12 that we would be *"lead forth with peace."* So Jesus Christ, the Prince of Peace, directed our steps and opened the doors for us to walk through.

We had two young children, no congregation, no money, and no building, so we moved slowly. Step-by-step the Lord led us by His Spirit and confirmed His promises. We finally stepped out in faith in February 1981.

Nothing happened fast, but little by little we saw Jesus save, heal, and set-free many people. We lived frugally, but He was always faithful to take care of us. Today, 33 years later, we are still pastoring at this same church. God has built His church and blessed us with a beautiful facility, eight acres of prime land in the middle of town, 300 members, and we are totally debt-free. We look back and give praise to the Lord for the faithful guidance of the Holy Spirit.

Pastor Dave Kaufman and his wife, Jeanne, have been married for 39 years. They founded Holy Life Tabernacle in 1981 and are the authors of the new book, White-Knuckle Faith. *Pastor Dave has hosted 37 Pastors Conferences and has made numerous ministry trips to build up the Body of Christ across the United States, Canada, Philippine Islands, Brazil, Guatemala, West Africa, and India. Learn more about their ministry at www.holylifetabernacle.com.*

When God Speaks
Christine Kirkegaard

After about 60 years in ministry, I have found that God speaks in many ways. I will list the ones I have experienced.

1. Sometimes I ask a question and He answers in the spirit (in His still, small voice).

2. Other times I am reading the Bible and he lights up a scripture and I feel He is talking to me specifically.

3. On one occasion, I was reading a book on healing and He spoke (in the spirit) and said, "If you sow time into another ministry, I will bless your ministry in a special way." We did this and He blessed abundantly.

4. One time I made one of those "they never" statements and God said, "Oh, really?" Because I responded right he blessed me with more sales of gift shop items than usual.

5. I had an impression in my mind to buy a book for more than I usually would pay, but I obeyed and with the autograph the author offered, he put a prophecy of "extra ordinary miracles," which came to pass in a big way within two months. They are still continuing.

6. Another time God spoke in a vision after I asked a question and gave an answer.

7. Sometimes I need a maintenance miracle (in my home) and I ask the Lord for help and that still, small voice says a few words and I obey and the problem is fixed and I am amazed that He cares about little things. Don't hesitate to ask. He loves you much more than you think.

I have never heard an audible voice but it is just as real when it comes in the spirit. We recognize our Father's voice.

Christine Kirkegaard has been in ministry for nearly sixty years. At age 88 she is still answering the call as the director of the Holyland Exhibit and president of the Holyland Bible Knowledge Society, located in Minneapolis, Minnesota. They have hosted over 100,000 visitors for tours through the years. Today, Christine still makes appointments for tours of the Holyland Exhibit in Minneapolis.

This is an excerpt from her book, Glory Stories, *reprinted with the author's permission. You can reach her by telephone at (612) 871-7444 for a tour appointment , or to purchase a copy of her book.*

Angel on an Airplane
Judy Linton

Eight years ago I was visiting family in Ohio. As my siblings and I have aged, it seemed like every year when I visited someone was in the hospital. I am the second youngest and my older siblings have had a lot of health problems.

At that time, my sister Phyllis was in the hospital and was very sick. The doctor told her that she was dying. After visiting with her and her children, I thought it would be best if I came back home and ask for time off from work. I thought I would be returning to Ohio for a funeral.

My flight back to Minneapolis was scheduled for 2:00 in the afternoon, and my sister-in-law took me to the airport. I checked my luggage and while I was waiting, my nephew came to the airport and said, "Judy, I don't think you should go."

At that moment I had a decision to make. *What should I do?* I thought. I had a clear feeling that I was to return home to Minnesota, in spite of my nephew's plea. So I told my nephew, "I think I will go on home and come back next week."

I boarded the plane and was seated next to a lady from Montana. I had a book out and she asked me what I was reading. I told her, but to this day I don't remember what I was reading. I was weeping as I answered.

Her question started a conversation and I told her that my sister was dying. She just happened to be a Christian counselor. What were the chances of that happening? She prayed and talked to me for the entire two-hour flight to Minneapolis, which was a bumpy one. I am not comfortable flying under normal circumstances, but I was so at peace visiting with her. I call her "my angel." As we were walking up the ramp, she said she would pray for my sister.

That night at the hospital, my sister Phyllis started to improve and lived for six more years. I believe that encounter on the plane was a divine appointment and led by the Holy Spirit. I was to go home so I could meet my angel on the plane. She was a comfort to me at that time in my life. And because of her prayers and those of many others, Phyllis was healed. I weep when I think of that encounter.

In Hebrews 13:2 (NKJV) the Bible says: *Do not forget to entertain strangers, for by so doing some have unwittingly entertained angels.*

I have never seen this woman again, nor do I remember her name or what she looks like. And that's okay. God knows. He sent me an angel and I am forever grateful.

Judy Linton grew up in tough circumstances and was saved as a teenager in a Salvation Army ministry outreach to her neighborhood. Although she was a believer for many years, she never truly experienced a deep relationship with God until nearly 50 years later when she met Jesus in a powerful way at a women's retreat. Everything began to change as she allowed the Holy Spirit to transform her. Since that time, she has gone on her first mission's trip, served as a women's ministry leader at her local church, taken Bible College classes, and become a licensed minister with RAIN Ministries. She is excited about her faith, ministers to the broken-hearted wherever she finds them, and loves Jesus with all her heart.

God Moved When I Wasn't Looking
Melissa Olson

A few years ago, I was working as general manager of a restaurant, had a part-time internship-turned-job as marketing director for a local non-profit, and was finishing my last semester at Northwestern College in St. Paul, Minnesota. Life was a balancing act to say the least.

As my college career was coming to an end, I was moving toward accepting my non-profit marketing job as my full-time career. The position couldn't have been more perfectly written for me unless they had actually stated, "Looking for a blonde-haired, blue-eyed, college grad that has worked for us for two years."

Over the next few weeks, I prayed hard to make God understand that this was the best path for my life. But after weeks of being talked to like the position was already mine, the founder announced that they were going to open the position to the public in order to follow the equal opportunity rules. My heart sank.

The Holy Spirit spoke with a simple, *"Be patient, My beloved."*

Within about a week of the job posting, they had hired a girl who had spent the last year in the Peace Corps; she had a marketing degree but no experience. Letting me know that her humanitarian efforts were greater than mine, the company had me spending the last three weeks of my employment training her in on all the systems that I had created. Teaching someone how to navigate Microsoft Excel, Word, and Adobe Photoshop felt like a strong kick in the gut. I was so mad at God, I couldn't imagine that He could have had any other plans for me. My heart was set on this ministry for Him. What was He thinking? Didn't He understand that I was doing this for Him?

Again, The Holy Spirit told me, *"Patience, My beloved."*

With no other job prospects on the horizon, I begrudgingly became full-time at my restaurant job. I did love the family I had made there and the money was great, so the long hours were tolerable. Soon, my general manager position morphed into general manager, catering and fundraising manager, and restaurant marketing pro.

Constantly working 12-hour shifts 10-14 days in a row began to weigh on just about every part of my life. I didn't have time for friends, family or church. I would sleep with all the down time I had, I was irritable, and I wasn't taking care of myself. In the seven years that I had been there, I hadn't gained much more than a few pounds, but the constant struggle of being stressed and always being around comfort food made that change quickly. In a year and a half of working myself like this, I had gained about forty pounds. My life was beginning to hit a wall.

On January 17, 2009, I was hosting a fundraiser for a local Christian elementary school at the restaurant. One of the kids attending was the daughter of a very good friend of my family, Janet Perrin (the author of this Bible study). When she had come to pick up her daughter, we were able to chat for a few minutes. She said there was a Kenyan missionary doing intercessory prayer at church that night and asked if I would like prayer for anything. Immediately I said, "PRAY ME OUT OF HERE!" The money was no longer worth the strife it was causing my life. She encouraged me with the story of how God kept Paul in prison until the right moment so that he would be used the way God had planned. We briefly prayed together in the parking lot, asking God to open His new door of opportunity. With the promise of someone praying for my life, I got back to work.

"Patience," I heard.

Three days later, an employee of our local Curves (my former gym and where I had also worked for a short time) walked through the door for lunch. We did the customary, barely-scratching-the-surface greeting, "Hello, how are you, what are you up to?" But I could tell there was something bothering her, so I asked. She told me how, after eight years in the community, the current owner couldn't handle the responsibility of Curves anymore because of some life circumstances and, unless a miracle happened, she would be closing at the end of February. My stomach lurched.

"Patience," came to mind once again.

I knew I had to go offer my condolences, but I chalked up my uneasiness to the connection I had made during the years I had been a member. I loved Curves and the friendships I had with members and the staff. I loved the program, I believed in the program, and I loved the results!

On my break that afternoon, I walked across the parking lot, wondering what exactly I was going to say to my former boss.

We talked about all the issues she was going through and how, after two years of trying to sell the club, she couldn't handle it anymore. Her heart wasn't in a position to give Curves the attention it needed to thrive. She had spoken with dozens of interested people, but had never felt comfortable handing over to them the business she had built. She was out of options. And this time, the Holy Spirit was silent for me.

I went back to work, my mind reeling from the idea that this might be my answer. I knew that I had always said that owning my own business would be an option someday, but a fitness club? Didn't God see how unfit I was? I was living an unhealthy lifestyle, I was up to my eyeballs in student loan debt, and when have I had any experience for this?

"Be still My beloved."

"Oh good you do hear my thoughts, so can you please explain why in the world I am even interested in this!?"

There was silence.

After work, I went back over to Curves to talk to the owner about what exactly it might take to own the business. Within the hour I had a paper full of ideas about monthly costs, payroll, legal papers the state needs, etc. I left with a peace in my spirit and a head frantically going over everything I might be considering. My business name had even come to mind immediately: Joie de Vivre, which means "the joy of life" in French. I had very little time to make a decision to move forward. I spent the night praying.

"*Trust Me,*" was God's reply.

The following day as I drove to work, I noticed my mind wandering. "Come on God, I need an answer here! I'm not cut out for this, but I'll do it if You want me to. But I really, really need an answer quick!"

I caught myself making deals with God, "I need a sheep skin like Gideon in the book of Judges. Make the next light green or red depending on what you want me to do!"

"*Trust Me,*" He said again.

"Then tell me where to turn."

The Curves owner was waiting for me in the restaurant when I walked through the door. She had papers in hand and a message from corporate saying that they would expedite my application and waive my fees. She had tears in her eyes when she told me, "I knew last night, even though you are just 23 years-old, I could not feel more comfortable giving my baby away." She sold me the business, the furnishings and all the equipment for just $1.00.

On April 20, 2009 I became the youngest sole proprietor the company has had. As I look back, I see where the doors were closed and how each job position I had held since I was 16 years-old was the Holy Spirit pointing me and preparing me for what God has made me for.

Melissa Olson graduated from Northwestern College in Roseville, Minnesota. She is active in her home church in Eagan, Minnesota and remains the owner of Curves of Chanhassen. Follow her at www.healthtodayhopetomorrow.com.

Finding God in a Bakery
Ronald Olson

The leading of God had been expressed in many different ways in my life, but I had never before sought direction for such a big step of faith.

I had been asked to partner with John Halvorsen in a ministry he was calling Prayer Walk America. God had directed him to prayerwalk the length and breadth of America. The walk from the Canadian border to the Gulf of Mexico had already been completed, and the final walk from the Pacific Ocean in Oregon to the Atlantic Ocean in Delaware was about to begin. This time, God was calling me to take my family out on the road with John as he walked.

This would be no small undertaking. My wife and I would have to get an RV to live in on the road, and we were going to take our kids out of school to join us. The big question was: How was this going to be possible?

We had a comfortable home that, of course, came with a mortgage and regular bills that had to be paid. Now, we were being asked to add the cost of living on the road, during which time there would be no regular income. Neither my wife nor I could figure out how to make this work, so we began to pray, "Lord, how are You going to take care of us?"

We continued to pray, but it was now just three weeks before the start of the walk and there was still no answer.

One morning, after I had delivered some work to a printer for our church, I felt like stopping for a doughnut. It was one of those wet, sloppy, February mornings in Minnesota. I parked the van, walked into the bakery, and was greeted by the man behind the counter. I didn't know him, but we chatted for a minute while I tried to decide what to get. As I looked up from the bakery case, he was looking past me out the window.

"Is that your van out there?" he asked.

I replied that it was.

"Why don't you drive it around to the back?" he urged.

I didn't understand that at all, and muttered something to the effect that I really just wanted a doughnut.

"No, just drive around back," he said again. And he disappeared through the swinging doors behind the counter.

I was standing all alone in the bakery and wasn't sure what to make of this. But with a shrug of my shoulders (and without my doughnut), I turned to the door, went outside and got in the van. I drove around the corner and turned into the alley leading to the bakery. As I parked next to the trash cans, the bakery door opened and out stepped this man.

He was carrying a big white bakery box and two grocery bags. The box was filled with all kinds of pastries and sweet rolls. The bags were overflowing with fresh-baked breads and rolls.

He came up to my window and said, "I just feel I'm supposed to give these to you."

He put everything in the back seat, then he stooped down to pick up a bunch of snow in his bare hand and proceeded to wash the dirt off my windshield. Finally, with a smile and quick wave, he went back inside.

As the bakery door closed, I started to wonder what had just happened. I had never met this man before, and I certainly hadn't experienced anything like this. All of a sudden, the presence of God filled my van and He began to speak to me.

"You've been asking Me how I'm going to take care of you" God said. "*This* is how I'm going to take care of you."

I began to weep.

Suddenly this step of faith we had been considering didn't seem so big anymore. I really had heard God's call those many weeks ago. And He had heard our prayers and answered in a way that couldn't be misunderstood.

Throughout the remaining time in that ministry, God's guidance was sure, His blessings were many, and His promise to take care of us was demonstrated time and time again.

Ronald Olson is a licensed minister, speaker, teacher and writer. He has worked with churches throughout the United States, helping them reach their communities for Christ. He is currently a Pastoral Elder of his home church in Eagan, Minnesota. Contact him at prayerwalk@yahoo.com.

Obedience Leads to a Miracle
Janet Perrin

In the spring of 2011, I brought my daughter and her teenage friends from our church youth group to a Minnesota Women's Conference for the Assemblies of God. A Christian singer by the name of Kari Jobe was in town and I had purchased tickets for my older daughter. I really wanted to go to another conference that was in town that weekend, but after praying about it for several days, I felt very specifically led to go to the A/G event.

I remember being very tired that night because I had gotten up early to watch the royal wedding of Princess Kate and Prince William with my two daughters, Hannah, then age 14, and Julia, then age 11. By the time the concert rolled around, which was about a 45 minute drive from our home, all I wanted to do was sleep. We got to the concert and I was nearly falling asleep on one of the pews in the church, when I decided to sit up (lest I should totally fall asleep). The moment I did, I noticed a man with a camera with a very long lens taking photos of the concert. I didn't know him well, but recognized him to be the founder of a local Christian radio station, Praise FM 95.3, which I listen to regularly. I had met him and his wife previously at conferences, but I didn't really know him at all.

When I looked at the man, whose name is David McIver, I had a sudden understanding in my spirit that a man who worked at his radio station and had been terribly sick, would be healed. I had heard prayer requests for the sick man over the radio for several months. He was in his twenties and had recently had a terrible stroke and was hospitalized. I had prayed for that man several times, but couldn't remember his name. Also, I had not been thinking of him or his situation in recent weeks.

My eyes kept being drawn to David McIver during the concert, and I got a very distinct impression that his sick friend would be healed in such a way that he would "breathe on his own, swallow and eat solid food normally." The strong impression came to me over and over, to the extent that it was almost like I could "feel" (in a sense) a breathing tube being taken out of my own throat. I recognized that this was a Word of Knowledge from the Holy Spirit. (It was not something I had been thinking about.)

I started to sense a clear direction from the Lord that I was to share this with David. I felt that the Holy Spirit was strongly prompting me to give him a Bible verse from Isaiah 53:5 and tell him the very specific way that his friend would be healed -- no breathing tube, normal swallowing and that he would eat solid food again.

I started to sweat, thinking of approaching this man, who was almost a total stranger, to declare these things about his very sick colleague and friend. Immediately, fearful thoughts started to come to me that were contrary to the clear impression I'd had from the Lord. It was like I was in turmoil, not wanting to hurt David's feelings, or to say something that wasn't truly from the Holy Spirit. Terrible thoughts started assaulting my mind, like, *sure he's not going to need a breathing tube, because he's going to die.*

I recognized the negative thoughts as spiritual warfare, and determined to obey God. I wrote down the impression I had during the concert, hoping to slip a note in the glass jar on the Praise FM table and run out of the building without talking personally to David. I was afraid of being wrong and hurting him or giving him false hope for his friend's recovery.

Well, I woke up enough to enjoy the concert, and as we were leaving, who should I bump into but David. At that point, I had no choice. I knew I had to obey God. I simply reintroduced myself, and told him of the impression I'd had and asked if we could pray for his friend. He was only too glad to pray with me. I remember declaring that Alex (David told me his name) was going to breathe on his own, eat solid food and swallow normally. In the moment that I declared Alex's healing of these specific things, I had a sudden surge of faith and just "knew in my heart" that this was a Word of Knowledge from the Holy Spirit and that Alex would be healed.

It was uncomfortable for me, but I did it anyway. David just looked at me, smiled and said, "I like the direction this is going!"

I left feeling like, *Oh well, at least I obeyed you, God.*

I cannot say my faith remained very high, but at least I felt I'd obeyed, and God could do what He wanted with my prophetic prayer. I had also given David the note I'd written during the concert (when I was hoping I wouldn't see him) and it had my e-mail address on it.

The concert was on a Friday night and on the following Tuesday morning I was checking my e-mail before a Christian friend of mine named Deb came over to pray. I found an e-mail in my in-box from David McIver. It said that on Friday night when we were praying together, Alex had a sudden, dramatic improvement in the hospital, and they removed the breathing or feeding tube and that he began to eat and swallow. Wow! I just jumped up and yelled and praised God, right in front of my computer. David further explained in the e-mail that the Word of Knowledge I had shared with him were the EXACT things Alex's family (whom I do not know at all) had been praying for. Praise the Lord!

Many, many, many people had prayed for Alex. In this case, I believe that the Word of Knowledge that the Holy Spirit gave me at the concert and my subsequent prayer that night, somehow turned out to be one of the last prayers that released divine healing for Alex! God is so good.

When Deb got to my house, I told her the testimony (she had been at the concert too and knew what I'd done). I had Praise FM 95.3 (www.praisefm.org) on in the background while I told Deb about the e-mail I'd just received. Suddenly, we noticed what was happening on the air and started to listen.

About one minute after I reminded Deb about my Word of Knowledge and prayer for Alex, David McIver started to get choked up while on the air because Alex came walking into the studio for the first time in several months! He had to have another announcer cover for him, because he must have been crying and hugging his dear friend, Alex. Deb and I were overwhelmed and overjoyed to hear that Alex was healed! We praised God, knowing how good and great He is, and thanked Him for letting us be part of this healing testimony! We knew that the Holy Spirit was turning what the enemy had meant for Alex's harm, into a testimony to bring Himself glory! We prayed and prayed that morning for Alex's healing to be completed and for the whole staff at Praise FM 95.3. It really encouraged our faith!

Even though I just had a very little faith, and had to overcome fear to share the Word of Knowledge and pray in a public setting, God still used my prayer to help bring Alex's healing to fruition. What a blessing! God will use even a small amount of faith, when combined with obedience, to bring about His desired healing in people's lives.

This experience really strengthened my faith and encouraged me to be obedient when I receive specific words of knowledge for healing in the future. It was a real encouragement to David McIver, too. As of July 2011, Alex was back on the air on Praise FM 95.3 and only had minor remaining symptoms from the stroke. I later saw him speak publicly at a Praise FM banquet. Many people had prayed and God brought healing to Alex according to His timetable.

Janet Perrin is the author of this Bible study. You can read more about her on page 190 in this book.

Grace Has a Name
Janet D. Perrin

Grace has a name. What is it, you ask? It's Dorothy. Not the famous movie character of the same name from the Wizard of Oz. The Dorothy I write about has been a mentor of mine (and of many others) in life and ministry for a number of years. To me, she exemplifies what God's grace looks like in action, and what it means to walk with Jesus. Let me explain by sharing one small example.

By way of background, Pastors Alan and Dorothy Langstaff have been in ministry together for over 40 years. Now in their 70s, they are still pastoring a local church. Their years of faithful ministry have been lived out in the midst of personal challenges that would have caused most to give up and quit. While their accomplishments are many, the way I see God's grace through Dorothy is lived out in her everyday life.

Recently, we had a chance to catch up and pray over the phone. Dorothy was ministering to me from a hospital bed in her living room. She's had a physical condition over the past several years that was aggravated last fall with the onset of a medical condition known as PMR, which at that time was accompanied by severe, debilitating pain.

Medication and the grace of God have made it possible for her to become actively involved in the church again, but she takes advantage of phone calls to lie down and rest. In spite of this, we found ourselves laughing and praising God as she shared a testimony.

One of her favorite verses is Psalm 149:5-6, *"Let the saints be joyful in glory, Let them sing aloud on their beds, Let the high praises of God be in their mouth, And a two-edged sword in their hands."* She is determined to live that verse out, and with the help of the Holy Spirit, she does it.

As frequent doctor visits have become the norm for Dorothy lately, she has purposed to ask God, in prayer, to use her to encourage others wherever she goes. In one of her recent appointments at the clinic to have blood work done, one of her lab technicians asked, "How is it that you have such peace and joy compared to my other patients who are often stressed and anxious?"

Dorothy answered, "It's Jesus that makes the difference."

Since then she's had a number of opportunities to share and pray with the lab technician. Now when she goes to the clinic she is greeted with hugs of affection and a greeting, "Dorothy, I'm so glad you're here again today!"

On another occasion, on the way to the doctor appointment with her husband, she felt the Lord say, "You are going to have an opportunity to pray for the doctor today."

Knowing she couldn't be presumptuous, she waited to see what would happen. It wasn't long before the doctor said out of the blue, "I just have to tell you what's going on in my life. I have not been able to sleep and I've been very anxious."

He went on to explain some very critical things going on in his family. At that point, Dorothy knew exactly what she had to do. "Can I pray for you?" she asked and held out her hand to him. He put his hand in hers while her husband looked on. As she prayed, she began to cry tears of compassion for him and his family. The doctor truly appreciated her prayers and has since given a good report on the situation that Dorothy prayed about.

She shared these testimonies from the hospital bed in her home with such joy, that my faith was renewed and strengthened. My own troubles faded into the background as I renewed my prayer for God to use me to bring His love wherever I go. You see, God loves Dorothy's medical providers so much that He sent her to be an emissary of His love. God's grace has a name, and to me, one of those names is Dorothy.

How about you? Can you bring God's grace to someone along the road of everyday life today?

Pastor Dorothy Langstaff and her husband, Alan, moved to the United States from Australia in the early 1980s. They have two daughters and six grandchildren. They are currently pastoring a church in Chaska, Minnesota. She has written a wonderful book, Called Together, *about the ministry she and her husband Alan have had. You can learn more about it and their ministry at www.kairosmin.org.*

The Birds of the Air
Janet D. Perrin

On one warm summer's day, I was trying to pray as I sat outside on our back deck. Instead of concentrating on my prayer, I kept being distracted as my attention wandered again and again to the little birds coming to eat at our bird feeder.

I had been anxiously thinking about some financial matters, and was praying for wisdom. As I sat and prayed, the little birds just kept flying in to eat seeds from the feeder. They were so sweet. *Tweet, tweet*, they kept chattering. They flew about, blissfully unaware of my anxiety and consternation.

I wasn't feeling particularly spiritual that morning, but at least I was having fun watching the birds. Frustrated, I thought, *I can't even focus on prayer. All I can do is sit here looking at the birds!* But then, a Bible verse that I'd memorized kept coming into my mind. In my anxious state, I dismissed it as my own thinking. Finally, I decided that at least I could read the Bible.

I flipped open my Bible to no place in particular, and there was my answer. It was the very same verse that had been coming to mind. On the page before me were these words found in Matthew 6:26:

Look at the birds of the air, for they neither sow nor reap nor gather into barns; yet your heavenly Father feeds them. Are you not of more value than they?

Peace flooded my heart, replacing my own anxious thoughts as I realized that God had spoken!

Janet Perrin is the author of this Bible study. You can read more about her on page 190 in this book.

The Green Chair
Janet D. Perrin

My sheep hear my voice, and I know them, and they follow Me (John 10:27).

I have a favorite coffee shop located in a charming old farmhouse in the town we used to live in. I was a frequent customer for years before we moved, and I still am as often as I can be on the weekends. It is one of my most cherished places to quietly sit and read the Bible before the start of a busy day. When I lived just around the corner, I often went there in the early morning and got lost in the pages of my Bible amid the din of conversations and the smell of roasting coffee. I liked to do my reading before I went to my part-time job at the local church where I worked for a number of years.

One early morning, coffee cup in one hand and my Bible in the other, I was headed to the back of the coffee shop to find an out-of-the-way nook where I could read. I was intent on self-isolation that particular morning. As I proceeded out of the front room with all its clamor, through the middle room and toward the back, I had an unusual impression. "Go sit in the green chair."

That seemed odd, as I wasn't thinking anything of the kind. I had already passed a set of green chairs in the noisy front room and had no intention of sitting there. Again, the same impression came a second and a third time. "Go sit in the green chair," a small voice seemed to speak into my heart.

Now, I've walked with the Lord long enough and studied His Word carefully enough to pay attention to this kind of thing. I have known and experienced the still, small voice of the Holy Spirit. I made a quick mental assessment of the situation and realized it was unlikely to be my own idea, since nothing could be further from my own intention that day.

Obediently, but reluctantly, I turned around and headed back toward the crowded front room, seating myself in one of the two comfortable green chairs. I happily noted that the other chair was unoccupied. I dismissed the notion of the Holy Spirit's leading, attributing it to my own thoughts, and hunkered down to read.

I was happily engrossed in personal Bible study when a man came up and sat down in the other chair. I turned myself slightly away, wanting to protect "my" time and hoping to avoid even a polite "hello" to this stranger. Also, I would not normally engage in conversation with an unknown man based upon my personal boundaries.

It wasn't long before the man interrupted me with an unusual statement that caught me off guard. Instead of a polite small-talk greeting, the stranger declared, "You're just like my wife!"

What? I thought to myself. He obviously ignored my body language and went on, "She's always reading the Bible, too."

It began to dawn on me that this was a person to whom God intended me to speak. *So that's why I was supposed to go and sit in the green chair*, I thought. Resigning myself to the loss of what I perceived to be "my" time, I patiently listened and answered while this total stranger proceeded to fire Bible questions at me, one after the other. It turned out to be a rather lively and engaging conversation. I ended up suggesting that perhaps he would enjoy reading the Bible as much as his wife did. He said he would consider all that I said.

During the course of our exchange, I became certain that it was in response to his wife's prayers for her unbelieving husband that I had been guided by the Holy Spirit to the green chair before he arrived. I was in the right place at the right time to answer his questions. I never saw him again, but trust that God used me as one who helped him along in his journey toward faith.

That day, I had walked with Jesus on the road of everyday life to a green chair in my local coffee shop. What a delightful reminder to know that God is busy answering prayer, and that I got to play a part in this one!

Janet Perrin is the author of this Bible study. You can read more about her on page 190 in this book.

A Divine Appointment by the Sea
Lisabeth Rebney

One summer evening while I was in Jamaica for a short-term mission trip, my group members wanted to make the three-block walk to the seawall to watch the sunset. It had been a long day getting acclimated to the heat and humidity, and I was tired. All I wanted to do was put my feet up. But the entire group was going, so I decided I would go, too.

While trying to think about how this would be fun, one of the group members said, "You never know, maybe the Lord has a divine appointment waiting for you at the wall."

That sentence she spoke to me was a Word of Knowledge. The instant she spoke it, I knew in my spirit that God had a plan and a purpose for me to go to the seawall that evening. I began to pray over that word, asking for guidance and protection, and praying that His name would be glorified.

When we got to the seawall, the group was sitting down watching the clouds gently come together to frame the setting sun. As we were making small talk, a man approached me and kindly asked me whether he could show me what he had been working on. He told me his name was Shango. I knew he was trying to sell me that necklace, but I listened anyway as he told me the meaning of the Rastafarian (a non-Christian religion) colors.

As he paused, I interjected that I had something I wanted to show him. It was called *The Wordless Book*. I explained the significance of the colors that represented the Good News, and he began to ask questions. Seeds of truth were being planted in Shango's heart. This was the divine appointment Jesus had planned!

Suddenly, a very tall man came right up in front of me and started yelling. He said some things in English and some in Patois (a Jamaican language that comprises words of the native languages of the many races). I didn't understand it all, but the message was clear! Hatred of the Gospel had overcome this man. As he continued to yell, a crowd started to gather to see what was going on. It was clear that this man's anger would escalate from a verbal outburst to a physical one. I knew he wanted to strike me!

As soon as he came up to me, I began to pray in the spirit. I knew God would tell me whether to stay or flee. Peace that surpassed the situation and natural understanding came over me, and I could see with my spiritual eyes the angel of the Lord between me and the man. Instantly, Psalm 91 came to my mind. I knew He had given His angels charge over me. Jesus reminded me that our battles are not against flesh and blood, as it tells us in Ephesians 6. This angry man in front of me was being used by the devil to try to steal, kill and destroy the work of the Gospel. The Lord told me to stay and resist the devil, and he would have to flee. Just as quickly as that man appeared, he suddenly stopped his outburst and walked away.

By this time the sun had set. Everyone in my group had missed seeing the orange sun sink below the horizon. They were in a hurry to leave this tense situation, and gathered around me so we could all go back to the place we were staying.

During the entire time the man was angrily yelling, I could see Shango standing behind him. God had urged me in my spirit to go back to Shango and tell him it was no mistake I went to the seawall that night. I explained to him that I hadn't wanted to go, but Jesus wanted him to know that He loves him. Seeds of truth were planted in Shango's heart. As we walked away, we saw nearly 100 people watching us. I realized Jesus had planted seeds in many hearts that night.

The hardest thing for me that night was whether I should pray for that angry man. He was filled with an intense hatred of Jesus. In His kind and gentle way, God reminded me of a man filled with intense hatred, who persecuted Christians for fun. This man was chosen by God, came to repentance, was filled with the Holy Spirit and went on to write a huge part of the New Testament. The testimony of Paul (Saul) encouraged me to pray for that angry man from the seawall to come to know the gentle and loving Jesus Christ as his Savior.

Lisabeth Rebney, along with her husband and children, resides in the Twin Cities area of Minnesota. Her deep love for Jesus and the spreading of the gospel has led her on mission trips both nationally and internationally. Lisabeth has a heart to see individuals personally introduced to the Lord, receive all that He has to bless them with, and to reach the world for Christ. She also leads the prayer ministry team at her local church. You can reach her at blessedtodeclare@gmail.com.

The Birth of a Book
Wilma Rich

Our Daddy in Heaven wants to communicate with all of His children today, just as He did in the Garden of Eden with Adam and Eve. When Jesus came, He declared the Father to us and restored our communication. One of the ways the Lord spoke to me recently was in a dream.

I received the first few lines of a story three times in three separate dreams one night. I remember waking after each one and repeating to myself what the Lord had said. The next morning I wrote down those words and then asked the Lord for more revelation. What unfolded over the next five or six days became the story of a "little seed" that was planted by the Divine Gardener and how the Gardener brought that seed into his destiny.

Upon reading the story to my children and grandchildren, they all encouraged me to get it published. Not knowing anything about this process, God led me to a publisher, but then I needed an illustrator. I didn't know anyone that fit that description. However, my daughter had just that week ministered with a gal who is a fantastic sculptor and, being an artist, she knew someone who might be interested in illustrating my book.

It turned out that this beautiful, gifted Christian woman was available and interested, and began to put form and color to my book, *Little Seed's Destiny: A Story of Trust and Growth*. The results were fantastic.

Prior to this adventure, the Lord had given me some little stories when I was reading the Bible, but I never dreamed of having a book published. Now I have several titles in my head that He's given me, and a book about a "little caterpillar" is on its way to life.

God is good all of the time and He has destinies for each of us that today, we may have no awareness of. However, if you choose to look at each day (and night) with expectancy, you will be amazed at what He wants to reveal to you about your destiny!

Wilma Rich is a retired biology teacher and loves God's magnificent Creation. She is the mother of two married children who love the Lord and 17 beautiful grandchildren that bring her great joy. She and her husband, Larry, have been married over 50 years. They are active in ministry together through The Family Restoration Project. To contact her or learn more about her book, go to www.familyrestorationproject.com.

The Shout of God, The Whisper of God, and The Highest Level of God's Guidance
Rev. Ramona Rickard

As a young mom with five kids, I had been very sick for several years. The very concerned medical doctors did all that they could do. I lived in pain every day and was on lots of medication, including pain pills and digestive enzymes laced with belladonna, a narcotic. We attended the Lutheran Conference on the Holy Spirit where I was powerfully and wonderfully healed of three very serious diseases: Lupus, Pancreatitis, and Thrombophlebitis.

Immediately after being healed, I could eat normally and my medical doctors were amazed! I was pain-free for the first time in 11 years and all my internal organs that had been swollen and inflamed became healthy. I no longer needed any of my medications and was completely well. That changed the very direction of our lives as we were invited to go to many places to share the testimony of my healing and to pray for the sick.

We found a Charismatic church and sat under the amazing teaching gift of our pastor. We dug deep in God's Word and had a great a hunger for His Presence. Along with a small group of sold-out believers, we had passionate commitment to prayer. In the atmosphere of that wonderful "Spiritual Hot House," we experienced rapid spiritual growth and soon were teaching the "Walk in the Spirit" class and leading a Home Group.

One day, after getting the kids off to school in the spring of 1975, I had an amazing experience. I was praying while doing the dishes, and was caught up in worshipping the Lord. With my hands in the warm water, I was singing with my whole heart focused on my love for Him and I looked out my kitchen window. There, coming out from between the pine trees in the woods that divided our yard from the neighbor's yard, I saw Jesus! To my absolute surprise, He walked from the ground right through the air, and I was stunned when He came face to face with me, coming right through the window and wall into my kitchen!

He did not speak words to me, but He spoke into my mind. He showed me a little boy who looked to be nine months old. He was wearing little yellow stretchy PJ's, and his mother was carrying him into the sanctuary at church through the double doors. Suddenly I could see right inside his skull, as if it were some kind of a science movie, and I watched as the Lord showed me how he had a lesion on his brain. I could see the electrical impulses hit that lesion, and how the electricity would misfire and scatter. He told me that this little boy was having 300 seizures a day, and that He wanted to heal him.

I hardly got my breath, and then He showed me inside a woman's knee and I could see that the cartilage was all damaged and torn. There was so much arthritis in her knees that she could hardly walk and was scheduled for surgery, but the Lord wanted to heal her, too! I was undone, but drawn in by feeling the depth of His emotions, His love, great mercy, and a deep compassion for their sufferings.

Next, He showed me inside a man's back, and showed me that the man was a truck driver. He had lifted a heavy box and had torn muscles and damaged nerves in his back and had several damaged discs. He was in such terrible pain that none of the pain meds worked for him. I could feel the Lord's anguish over these situations.

I was so overcome by His presence that I fell to my knees, embarrassed that Jesus, my Lord, had come into my messy kitchen. I crawled through the dining room into the living room and knelt in front of my "prayer chair" where I spent time with the Lord each day. I put my face in my arms and wept and trembled! By this time the whole visionary experience was over.

Just then the phone rang. It was my husband Jim, calling from work. Hearing my voice, he became concerned and asked if I had been crying. I tearfully told him what I experienced as he was trying to calm me down. I tried to compose myself, but all my circuits were blown!

Jim continued to calm me and reassure me that this was a good thing, and he had the common sense to tell me to write it all down. He said that it was a word from the Lord, a Word of Knowledge, one of the gifts of the Holy Spirit in I Corinthians 12. Still catching my breath, and at times just staring out into space, I tried as hard as I could to write it all on a punch card that I had tucked in my Bible.

A week and a half went by, and having forgotten all about my experience, I had gone on with life as usual. At the Friday night Prayer and Praise meeting, Pastor Don Pfotenhauer preached on the Healing of the Paralytic, from Luke 5. At the end of the story, Jesus perceives what the Pharisees were thinking, and He says to them, *"Why are you reasoning in your hearts? Which is easier to say, 'Your sins are forgiven you,' or to say, 'rise up and walk?' But that you may know that The Son of Man has power on earth to forgive sins"- He said to the man who was paralyzed, "I say to you, arise, take up your bed and go to your house." Immediately he rose up before them, took up what he had been lying on, and departed to his own house, glorifying God, and they were all amazed, and they glorified God. And were filled with fear, saying "We have seen strange things today!"* (In other words, "We have never seen anything like this before!")

When Pastor Don said that, suddenly that which had been locked away in my heart all flooded back! I pulled the card out of my Bible, waving it wildly in the air and saying "Pastor Don, Pastor Don, read this!"

He asked me to read it, but perceived how frightened I was. He called me up front and asked again for me to read it while he steadied me with an arm around my shoulder.

I read it while I was shaking like a leaf. Then I quickly took my seat and came under the condemnation of the enemy of our souls. "You just made a fool of yourself! That was the stupidest thing you have ever done! They all think that you are crazy!"

I was weeping profusely when someone came and tapped me on the shoulder and said, "Look!"

There, coming through the double doors, was the woman that I saw in the vision! She was dressed just like I saw her in elephant bell blue jeans. She had long curly hair parted in the middle, love beads around her neck, and she was carrying the little boy. His name was Isaiah, and was the size of a nine-month-old, but was actually three years old. He was born with Cerebral Palsy, and his mother said, "He has 300 seizures a day!"

She said that she had a baby girl the night before who was being cared for in the crying room. Due to lack of medical insurance she was unable to stay in the hospital, so her ex-husband came and brought her and the new baby girl home and helped her. When she woke up in the morning, she heard the voice of the Lord telling her to bring her little boy to Way of the Cross Church.

She had never heard of Way of the Cross, and had to look it up in the telephone book and call for directions. Pastor Don asked if Jim and I would come up and pray for her little boy. I said that there was one more thing. It was not written down on my card, but the Lord had shown me that there needed to be reconciliation between the mom and dad, and then He wanted to heal the boy. He showed what a strong protection it is for children to have a mother and father in covenant together with Him. The mother said, "He is back in the crying room with our new baby girl."

A couple of the men went back to get him and bring him in, and he came quickly, carrying the beautiful one day old baby. We shared with them what the Lord wanted to do, and feeling the holy Presence of the Lord, they both recommitted their lives to Him and to one another. They embraced, holding their children in their arms. We prayed for the little boy and the peace of God came on the whole little family.

There was such a high level of faith in the sanctuary that night, that the older woman I saw in my vision came up with great expectancy. Her name was Julianna. She had a double knee replacement set for the following Monday morning. We prayed for her, God touched her, and she was totally healed. All glory to God!

Then Art, the truck driver from the vision came up and shared that his injuries were just exactly as I had read them off the card that had been tucked in my Bible. He had no doubt that God would heal him after what he had just witnessed.

Three weeks later I saw little Isaiah's father at a celebration at the church. He was darting down the staircase from the foyer to the church basement. I hollered down the steps, "Hey, you're Isaiah's father aren't you?"

"Yep, I sure am," he shouted back.

"How's he doing?" I called.

"He's doing great! He has not had a seizure since you and your husband prayed for him!"

Wow! How awesome that was. We saw Julianna quite often when she would visit our church with her son and his family. She never had to have that surgery and her knees served her well without pain. And Art, well, every time I saw him over the ensuing years he would always say, "My back is still healed!"

Sometimes God gives us instruction with a loud voice, a shout! That experience was a "shout from God!" It was important and He was teaching me. I knew nothing about Words of Knowledge, and Jim had to explain the experience to me. I have had God shout to me only a few times over these nearly 40 years, but as I have grown in understanding His Word, and have grown in a more intimate relationship with Him, He most often speaks with a whisper.

Psalm 32:8 says, *"I will instruct you and teach you in the way you should go; I will guide you with my eye.*"

The Space between the shout of God and His guiding you with His eye is made shorter by:

1. Drawing near to the Lord (intimacy)

2. Growing in faith (trusting Him to speak to you and lead you)

3. The level of obedience (responding to Him immediately)

Jesus walked into my house that day in an eyes-wide-open vision and gave me that incredible, life-altering revelation. In His timing I stepped into it, afraid, but willing to be a fool for Christ, AND AMAZING THINGS HAPPENED!

Ramona Rickard is an ordained minister and, along with her husband, Jim, pastored for a total of 37 years. They are the founders of RAIN an Apostolic Network of Pastors, Churches, Trans-Local Ministers and Missionaries. They also are founders of The International Association of Healing Ministries. Together they are following God's mandate to "restore the power of the Holy Spirit to the Church of Jesus Christ." They travel to the nations of the world teaching pastors to do the works of Jesus, and do large evangelistic Healing & Miracle Festivals. They have 5 grown and married children, 13 grandchildren, and 4 great grandchildren. For more information on Pastor Ramona's ministry, visit www.rainministries.org.

This story is an excerpt from Ramona's soon-to-be published book, The Day The Angels Came: A Wonder-filled Account of Heaven's Collaboration with Believers on Earth.

One More Time
Paul Ridgeway

On a recent Christmas I was the guest of a businessman who, along with several of my close friends, was hosting a dinner to celebrate my birthday. This man owns several service stations in the Twin Cities and he and his wife are wonderful Christians.

While at dinner that night in their home, they were telling the story of an employee of theirs who had walked into their office the day before Christmas. (This couple, as well as others, had witnessed to this man many times, but he still wasn't a Christian.) When he walked into the office, he started talking and then began to mumble and suddenly fell to the floor. At first they thought he was dead, but he had suffered a major stroke and was completely paralyzed. He was only 59 years-old.

As I listened to their story, I felt led to immediately suggest that we go see him in the hospital to tell him about Jesus one more time. I knew that it's not God's will that any should perish. Proverbs tells us that God gets no joy in the death of the wicked.

We were able to arrange to see him on the second morning after our dinner. I met the couple this man worked for and we rode together to the hospital. When we entered his room, we found him in a coma and unable to move any part of his body. My friends spoke to him for several minutes, not knowing if he could hear them.

When they told him that I was in the room with them, I walked up to the bed and began to speak to him. I asked the Holy Spirit to reach this man that he might have at least one more chance to come to a saving knowledge of Jesus. I told him that I felt God had brought me to him to tell him about the love of Jesus and how he could receive eternal life through Christ. I asked the Holy Spirit to awaken him to hear the gospel of Jesus Christ.

As I laid my hands on him and told him Jesus sent me, the man's whole body jumped up in bed. My two friends were shocked and excited about what God had done and was going to do. I presented the gospel to this man and asked him to make a decision about receiving Jesus as his Savior. I knew he had done it, even if he couldn't speak, because the Holy Spirit had allowed him to hear me and be open one more time to receive Christ. My friend then asked him to squeeze his finger if he had heard my witness to him and if he had accepted Jesus as his Lord and Savior. The man squeezed his employer's finger, even though medically, he was not supposed to be able to move any part of his body.

The man laid back in bed and I knew that only the God of heaven could have done this. I knew this man was born-again. About one week later he passed away. But because God led us to go visit him and share the gospel, we know that he passed into the waiting arms of Christ. Praise the Lord!

We all need to be concerned about the lost and be willing and ready to witness whenever the Holy Spirit speaks to us.

Paul Ridgeway is the president of Ridgeway International, which creates special events for such corporate clients as the NFL, the United Way, The Salvation Army, NCAA, Coca-Cola, and many others. His real love is evangelism, and has spo-

ken in churches and to groups across the United States. His seminar, Tell Them, Because Eternity is Forever, *trains and equips Christians on how to witness to people about Jesus Christ.*

Currently, Paul is radio host of "On the Way with Ridgeway," *which airs on KKMS in Minneapolis-St. Paul, Minnesota. He and his wife, Rosalind, have been married almost 39 years. They have two children, a daughter-in-law, and one grandchild. For more information on his show or to contact Paul, go to www.kkms.com.*

Two Sandwiches
Rev. Damien Wong

Some time ago, one of the girls from YWAM (Youth With a Mission) who came to our church, woke up one morning and felt an impression from the Lord. "I want you to go down to Border's and buy a Canadian newspaper," she felt Him say.

Even though she was from Canada and would like to see the latest news, she began to argue with God. "But Lord, I don't want to go and buy a newspaper. I don't want to go to Border's or to buy a newspaper."

Immediately she felt the same impression again, and while she was battling with the Lord a little bit, she decided to obey. As she was about to leave the house, she decided to make a sandwich, but then she felt God impress her to make two sandwiches. She didn't feel extra hungry, but the impression was so strong (and she knew she wouldn't win an argument with God) she made two sandwiches.

When she got to Border's she found there was no Canadian newspaper that day. *I know I heard that I was supposed to buy a newspaper,* she thought. Puzzled, she walked out the door, turned a corner, and bumped right into a girl. This startled her and as she looked into the face of this girl, the first words out of her mouth were not "excuse me" but, "Do you want a sandwich?"

She didn't even know why she said it; it just popped out of her mouth. The girl replied, "Yes! Me and my boyfriend are hungry and we just said a short prayer for food, about a minute ago."

As my friend gave them the sandwiches she told them about our church and that we serve free meals on Wednesday nights. So the girl and her boyfriend came to church that night, and after eating she came down for prayer. She told me she had cancer in her ovaries, so I prayed for her and knew that God touched her, but I didn't know to what extent. I didn't see her again for over a year.

As I was ministering in another city about a year later, a girl came up to me and said, "Hi, do you recognize me? Do you remember me?"

I told her I didn't, and felt like I'd never seen her in my life, but she said, "Remember you prayed for me about a year ago and I got healed and I don't have cancer!"

She was so different. It was as if God had completely transformed her! Here was a beautiful young woman whom God had touched and had been healed of cancer, and it all began when my friend got an impression to go and buy a newspaper. Notice the Lord didn't say, "I want you to go down to Border's because you're going to run into this girl with her boyfriend and they're going to be hungry and so make two sandwiches." The Lord doesn't usually work that way. She simply knew that she was impressed by the Lord to go down to Border's and to bring two sandwiches. She just obeyed.

The Lord wants to use you in that way, as well. In 1 Corinthians 2:4 Paul writes, *"I don't come to you with persuasive words of man's wisdom but with demonstration of the Spirit and of power."* Each day ask the Holy Spirit to fill you and allow you to demonstrate Him. It's as easy as, "Holy Spirit fill me and help me demonstrate you out in the world in some way."

Do you think He'll answer that prayer? Of course He will. It's so much fun when you allow the Holy Spirit to use you and you demonstrate His power. All you need to do is say "Yes," and then just have fun with the Holy Spirit and fun with Jesus!

Rev. Damien Wong is Senior Pastor of Kona Life Church in Kona, Hawaii. He has been featured in Charisma *magazine, as well as on* Praise The Lord *and* Tender Touch *television shows. He ministers throughout the Hawaiian islands and internationally, and sees the supernatural power of God demonstrated wherever he goes. Pastor Damien's church website is found at www.konalifechurch.org.*

About The Author

Janet DeCaster Perrin, loves the Word of God and has a passion for equipping Christians and helping them to draw closer to Jesus by learning to be sensitive to His Holy Spirit. She is a wife and mother of two teenaged daughters.

Janet has served as a women's pastor, Bible college adjunct faculty member, global missions team member, ministry volunteer, and deacon at her local church. She holds a B.A. from the University of Wisconsin-Madison, a J.D. from Emory University School of Law, a Certificate of Biblical Studies from ACTS International Bible College, and received a ministerial license from Resurrection Apostolic International Network (RAIN).

She shares testimonies and teachings about walking with Jesus on the road of everyday life at her blog, **www.asamaritanwomanspeaks.com**.

Contact her at **asamaritanwomanspeaks@gmail.com** or on Twitter **@janetDCperrin**.

Additional Books

This book is available as a TEACHER MANUAL, a ready-made guide that enables anyone to train and disciple others in the truth of Holy Spirit-empowered living. Included is a complete version of the STUDENT MANUAL. Together, they provide all the tools needed to present this study in a small group, church Bible study, or Bible college classroom. The STUDENT MANUAL is also available separately.

For additional copies of this or other books by Janet DeCaster Perrin, contact the author at **asamaritanwomanspeaks@gmail.com**, or go to **www.amazon.com/author.janetdperrin**.

Photo Credit
The author's photo by Lindsay May at lindsaymayphotography.com.

Made in the USA
San Bernardino, CA
11 March 2016